SUPERSENSIBLE IMPULSES

IN THE HISTORICAL DEVELOPMENT OF HUMANITY

SUPERSENSIBLE IMPULSES
IN THE HISTORICAL DEVELOPMENT OF HUMANITY

Eight lectures held in Dornach from 16 September to 1 October 1922

TRANSLATED BY PAUL KING

INTRODUCTION BY DALE BRUNSVOLD

RUDOLF STEINER

RUDOLF STEINER PRESS

CW 216

Rudolf Steiner Press
Hillside House, The Square
Forest Row, RH18 5ES

www.rudolfsteinerpress.com

Published by Rudolf Steiner Press 2024

Originally published in German under the title *Die Grundimpulse des weltgeschlichtlichen Werdens der Menschheit* (volume 216 in the *Rudolf Steiner Gesamtausgabe* or Collected Works) by Rudolf Steiner Verlag, Dornach, based on shorthand notes that were not reviewed or revised by the speaker. This authorized translation is based on the third German edition (1988), edited by Ernst Weidmann

Published by permission of the Rudolf Steiner Nachlassverwaltung, Dornach

A catalogue record for this book is available from the British Library

ISBN 978 1 85584 663 0

Cover by Morgan Creative

Typeset by Symbiosys Technologies, Visakhapatnam, India
Printed and bound by 4Edge Ltd., Essex

Contents

Publisher's Note

These lectures, in which the essence of the cultic forms a central motif, receive their special significance on the one hand from the fact that they are to be seen in connection with the cultic activity which Rudolf Steiner himself carried out in the years 1906–1914 within the epistemological department of the Esoteric School (see Rudolf Steiner, *Zur Geschichte und aus den Inhalten der erkenntniskultischen Abteilung der Esoterischen Schule 1904–1914. Briefe, Dokumente und Vorträge*, GA Bibl. No. 265, *Freemasonry and Ritual Work*, SteinerBooks 2007), on the other hand by the fact that they were held in the same days in which The Christian Community was founded, for which Rudolf Steiner mediated the cultus.

Introduction

What must it have been like as a neophyte in the ancient mysteries, to sit at the feet of the great hierophant and be instructed; to be given the preparation necessary to enter into the spiritual worlds protected, filled with the strength to receive and understand all that the spiritual world then reveals? How must it have been to be removed, for a time, from one's day-to-day consciousness that is filled with the concepts awakened by the perceptions of the physical world, and be filled instead with concepts that have yet to experience their spiritually perceived counterpart in initiation?

In our time, we have the vast spiritual research of Rudolf Steiner – a research fit and appropriate for today – through which to begin our own preparation: either for the time after death or as the firm scaffolding through which to navigate our own spiritual development. In these eight lectures, begun on 16 September 1922 – the day of the inauguration of the soon-to-be worldwide organization known as The Christian Community, Movement for Religious Renewal – we experience the spiritual riches of a great hierophant of the modern age. Although not founded by Dr Steiner, The Christian Community, that he helped into being, became very dear to his heart. And, from the very start, the intensity of these lectures seems to suggest that that endearing sentiment might have been there from the very beginning, although these are not lectures about that Movement for Religious Renewal as such.

So, imagine the beginning of a worldwide movement – the hope, the excitement that would underlie it, in all who attended – and recall that Steiner always spoke to those present and not out of an abstract vacuum. Who was present mattered!

From the start, we are flung into the cosmic expanses of the spiritual worlds, carried up on the astral spirals rising out of the blossoms of the plant realm (yes, so it is said!). We are aided also by the 'negative' weight (that rises instead of falls) of the spiritual–ideal content of the mineral–metal world, directing us to various planets in the planetary spheres. We consider the constellations from the vantage point of the earth and the point-centredness of egohood, and then from the other side and the periphery nature of spirit consciousness. We encounter, upon reincarnation, the horizontal-like contentious passions of the group souls and are informed how important our relationship to Christ is in order to preserve one's destiny, as laid out by the spiritual hierarchies in spirit spheres.

In 1917, Rudolf Steiner published *Riddles of the Soul*, which brought forth the fundamental anthroposophical idea of the threefold human being. In the second of his lectures here, we see Steiner expanding on our relation to the three hierarchies in respect to the 'head system', the 'chest/rhythm system' and the 'limb/metabolic system'. The connections he establishes again point to the fruits of our lives lived, our busy time between death and a new birth, and the mutual relations of our moral fruits (good and bad) with our experiences of the spiritual hierarchies. Each part of us undergoes specific metamorphoses in the spiritual worlds. The head is a work of art, 'an image of something universal that is contracted and filled out with material existence' (p. 16).

One gets the impression here that Dr Steiner would like to bring to the celebrants of a new ritual an historical context, from out the spiritual world, as to what transpires spiritually in authentic celebration. What are the hidden aspects of most relevance, considering that Dr Steiner has such a vast panorama of spiritual facts that could be shared? There is the karmic reality of a life lived – and this a sacrament in every case – that raises up its fruits to the higher hierarchies via the head, chest and limb systems. Thus given over, they are worked upon and – in this work – the hierarchies evolve. In the transformation of a given life's thoughts, feelings and deeds, a new spirit seed is returned to the earth to again reap what it shall sow in a new incarnation.

In Lecture 3, we are introduced to the evolution of consciousness in a different way. Here, the ideas of inhalation and exhalation frame our relationship to the spiritual world. Through a predominance of inhalation in the Indian and Persian epochs, and the porous nature of sleep and waking in that time, we were able to receive revelation from the moon beings, through which civilization was guided. As this quality of consciousness began to fade but inhalation still prevailed, the moon beings only became available through darker forces, and so were no longer accessible in a healthy way. In a sense, they could find no shelter here until, in the Egyptian epoch, mummification led to a renewed capacity for communication with the moon beings, who could 'find shelter' in these human forms. And once again, the wisdom from the moon beings via Egyptian initiates could guide civilization.

By the time of the Greek and Roman civilizations, inhalation and exhalation achieved a balance that brought about a relationship to elemental luciferic beings. They half flew, half swam in the air, and this dance affected the way that music and poetry developed at that time. So, in the fourth and fifth centuries after Christ, we have another set of elemental beings finding a relationship to our ever-evolving consciousness. Whereas the earlier relationships to the moon beings in Indian and Persian times and the air demons of Greek and Roman times looked to the past, now we have a period where exhalation predominates and this new set of elementals, called 'earth being elementals', have arrived on the scene. This means that, since the fifteenth century, those who experience a moral idea can 'exhale' it into external cosmic life. This is the beginning of the creation of a foundation for the future Jupiter existence! But a hindrance to this mutual endeavour is our dogmatic adherence to the idea of heredity. Also, when these elemental earth-beings come upon machines – which only reflect ideas and are devoid of spirit – they are particularly horrified.

In Lecture 5, Rudolf Steiner again takes us through the ways that people of different epochs approached the spiritual worlds for guidance; how, in the Indian and Persian epochs, the spiritual world was more directly experienced through inhalation. Through the beings of the moon, wisdom was imparted through which civilization was guided. By the time of the Egyptian epoch, this orientation towards inhalation had faded, and for a period there was no way to continue to communicate with the moon beings – until the time of mummification! Here, albeit in a now decadent form, human souls were for a time bound to their mummified remains and, through this orientation, the moon beings – who otherwise could not find 'shelter' here – were again able to communicate with the Egyptian initiates. The Egyptian initiates were able to discover knowledge of the human being directly, but they could only come to an understanding of nature – of the mineral, plant and animal kingdoms – through the indirect method with mummies.

The Egyptians were otherwise unable to form concepts of nature, as we can now do after the Mystery of Golgotha. After Christ, our whole inward organization was changed and, when looking upon the world without revelations from the spirit, we ourselves began to take hold of the sense world with the newly arisen intellect. And yet in future this must become a spiritualized intellect, where the force in ideas can be transferred to our exhalation.

In this 'pregnancy', so to speak, we recapitulated the ancient mummification process, although this now took place through ancient rituals, primarily pre-Christian. In the fourteenth and fifteenth centuries, when the complete intellectualization of culture had come about, these ancient rituals were conserved in occult Orders. (It is interesting how one can get a sense here of what Dr Steiner refers to elsewhere, i.e. of how each epoch finds recapitulation in a later one – the first in the seventh to come, the second in the sixth, and here, the third, in our own fifth.) These preserved rituals are just as much 'mummies' in that they are not illumined and warmed through by the Mystery of Golgotha. And yet the spiritual beings can find a path to carry the exhalations into the etheric world through these somewhat problematic rituals.

But the modern individual needs something that can convey a knowledge of the spirit, a *spiritual science.* When a person is in the process of returning to new incarnation, they might visit the occult lodges that are not completely devoid of soul – and there they buzz and flutter in an existence that precedes their birth. Within the lodges, there might be those who can receive communications from these pre-birth souls. And such people feel the spiritual world and speak authentically in relation to it. We can see, in various writers, where the influences of these communications have been experienced.

In what way, perhaps, does the new (Christian Community) ritual of 'The Consecration of the Human Being' relate to our next steps in evolution? Now, once again, a living knowledge of the spirit strives to live in ritual. Is this a return of soul through which the elemental earth beings might carry the inner gifts of modern humanity out into the cosmic world?

We are regularly asked by Dr Steiner to extend our imagination toward the constant steadfast working of the spiritual worlds into the physical, in the sense of life being constantly maintained, consciousness being everywhere nurtured, and self-awareness ever evolving. And now, at the dawn of a new ritual brought out of the new mysteries founded by Rudolf Steiner, we are brought these lectures.

As the good Doctor Steiner has said elsewhere: '*For we are the religion of the Gods.*'

Dale Brunsvold
March 2024

Lecture 1

DORNACH, 16 SEPTEMBER 1922

THINGS to do with the spiritual world can be expressed in different ways and elucidated from different angles. They then sometimes sound disparate. But it is precisely through these varied elucidations that facts about the spiritual world can be presented in a complete form to the soul. And so this evening I will bring in a somewhat different language and different elucidation, certain things that I discussed in the last two lectures[1] given in the Goetheanum concerning human experience between death and a new birth.

We have heard that, when our physical body falls away, the human being goes over into a condition of cosmic experience. After separating from the physical body we still carry our etheric organism with us, but we no longer feel ourselves to be inside this etheric organism; we feel our soul spread out into the widths of the cosmos. However, we cannot yet distinguish with any clarity the beings and processes from each other in these widths of the cosmos, over which our consciousness now begins to expand. We have a cosmic consciousness, but this consciousness still lacks inner clarity. And in addition, this consciousness is initially absorbed during the first few days after death in the etheric body which is still present. The first thing to be lost is what in the human being is tied to our head-system (*Kopforganisation*). I'm not being ironic, but completely serious when I say that the very first thing we lose, also in a soul sense, when we pass through the portal of death, is our head. The head-system ceases to function.

Now, it is precisely the head-system that facilitates our thinking in earthly existence. It is by means of the head-system that people form their thoughts in a certain activity during earthly existence. The head-system is lost when we step through the portal of death, but our thoughts are not; our thoughts remain. But they are permeated by a certain inner 'aliveness'. They become dim, indistinct spiritual entities that direct us out into the widths of the cosmos. It is as though the thoughts had separated away from the human head, as though they still cast a backward light on the life just lived which we experience as our etheric organism, but as though at the same time they were pointing us towards the widths of the cosmos. We do not yet know what they want to tell us, these human ideas, that were yoked and penned up in the head-system, but are now freed and pointing to the widths of the cosmos.

When, for the reasons and in the way I described yesterday in the [Goetheanum] building, the etheric body has dispersed, when our cosmic consciousness is no longer tied by it to our last earthly life (in the other way which I described, it initially remains tied), when the etheric body has now also separated from the human being, then the thoughts which have torn free from the head-system become brighter, as it were, and we now notice how these ideas are pointing us into the cosmos, into the universe.

The way it works initially is that we go out into the universe through the mediation of the plant world. Please do not misunderstand me here: I am not saying that it is the plants covering the earth at the place where we die that prepare the way for us, but when we look at the earth's plant world, how it presents itself to our spiritual gaze is such that what our physical eyes see is only a part of the plant world. I will draw what happens in a diagram on the board [see drawing]. Assume that this is the surface of the earth, and plants are growing out of this surface [*grün* = green]. Of course, it's not drawn in proportion, but you will understand what I mean. We can follow these plants with our senses up to when they flower [*rot* = red]. But spiritual perception of plants shows that this is only part of the plant world and that from the flower upwards there begins a weaving of processes of an astral nature. There is an astral element that is as though poured out over the earth, and spiral-shaped structures arise from this astrality [*gelb* = yellow].

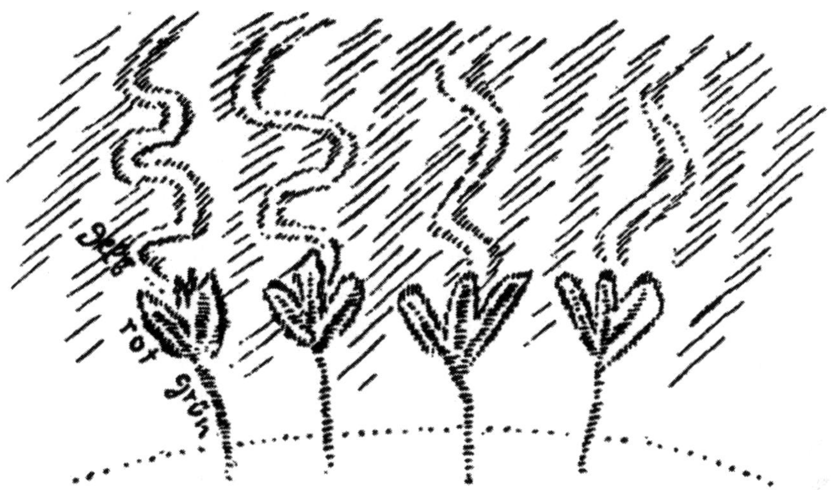

Wherever the earth makes it possible for plants to grow, the plants evoke a streaming out of these astral spirals.

These cosmic spirals surround the earth everywhere, so that we mustn't think that this streaming down, this glittering and gleaming of the cosmic astral spirals only occurs in places where plants grow. It is present in various ways everywhere. So someone might die in the desert and yet, as they flow out into the universe, still be able to meet these plant spirals.

The plant spirals are the path along which we move from the earth to the planetary sphere. Thus, by means of the spiritual extensions of the earth's plant world, we slip, as it were, out of the earthly realm. These become wider and wider. The spirals broaden out more and more, their circles becoming ever more expansive. They are our route out into the spiritual world. But we would not be able to go there, we would always have to remain stationary, as it were, if we did not receive the possibility of having 'negative' weights of a sort, weights that don't pull downwards but push us upwards. And these weights are the spiritual content, the ideas, of the mineral structures in the earth, particularly the metals. So we move along the courses of the plants into the widths of the cosmos, and are supported by the force of the earth's metals that carries us towards the planets. The quality of each mineral structure is such that its intrinsic idea always carries us to a particular planet. So we would say, for example, that minerals related to tin—that is, their ideas—carry us to a specific planet; that what is in the earth as iron—that is, the idea of iron—carries us to another specific planet. Thus, in their spiritual counter-images, the mineral and plant worlds that play a role for human beings in their environment during earthly existence, undertake after death to conduct human beings into the widths of the cosmos. And we are truly carried into the movements of the planets, into the whole rhythm of planetary movement, by the mineral and plant kingdoms of the earth.

By our consciousness gradually expanding over the whole planetary system, so that we are aware of this planetary life in the inner world of our own soul, we float through the entire planetary system. Were nothing else there but what pours forth into the widths from plant and mineral existence, we would experience in it everything that can be experienced in the mysteries of the plant and mineral kingdoms. And these mysteries are extraordinarily varied; they are great and stupendous, rich in content, and no one need believe that the life that now begins for the soul-spiritual person once they have left their physical organism is poorer than day-to-day life on earth. It is manifold, but it is also majestic. We can experience more in the mysteries of a single mineral than we experience in earthly life in all the kingdoms of nature put together.

But there is something else in this planetary sphere that we wander through. There are moon-forces, the spiritual moon-forces that we described a few days ago. The moon-sphere is there. But the more we live into existence beyond the earth, the weaker its influence becomes. Its influence is strong in the early period after death—which is to be reckoned in years. It becomes ever weaker the more our cosmic consciousness expands. If this moon-sphere were not present, there are two things we would not be able to experience after death.

The first is the entity I referred to recently. We have constructed this ourselves in the life just lived out of the forces comprising the moral and spiritual evaluation of our earthly life. We have constructed a spiritual entity, a kind of spiritual elemental being, whose limbs, whose tentacle-like structures are a reflection of our human moral-spiritual worth. If I may put it like this: the soul is accompanied by a living photograph, formed by the substance of the astral cosmos, but which is real and 'alive', a photograph in which we see what sort of person we actually were in our last life on earth. We have this photograph before us for as long as we are in the moon sphere.

But apart from this we also experience in the moon-sphere all kinds of elemental beings. We soon notice that these beings have a kind of dream consciousness—but a very bright dream consciousness—which alternates with a brighter state of consciousness, even brighter than human consciousness on earth. These beings alternate, as it were, between a dull, dreamlike state of consciousness and a consciousness that is brighter than that of people on earth. We become acquainted with these beings. They are very numerous and differ considerably from each other in shape. In the condition of life [after death] I am describing, we see these beings as floating down to earth when they enter their dull, dreamlike consciousness; how they are pushed down to earth, as it were, by the spirituality of the moon, and how they float back again.

We meet a rich life of these forms, floating down to earth and then back again, as I have described. We come to recognize that there is a relationship between these forms and the animal kingdom on earth. We come to recognize that these figures are the so-called group-souls of the animals. These animal group-souls come down; [when this happens] it means that a particular animal species wakes up down on earth. When the animal species enters a condition of sleep, the group-soul rises into the heights. In short, we notice that the animal kingdom stands in relationship with the cosmos such that the moon-sphere is the life-field for the group-souls of animals. Animals do not have individual souls; whole groups of animals [i.e. species], lions, tigers, cats, etc. have common group-souls. These group-souls lead their existence in the moon sphere, moving up and down. And the life of animals is influenced from the moon-sphere in this alternation of up and down.

It is simply a cosmic law that we have our moral-astral counter-image in the sphere where we encounter the animal group-souls—in other words, in the moon-sphere. For when we live further with our cosmic consciousness into broad expanses of the cosmos, we leave behind in the moon-sphere this living photograph, as I have described, of where we have got to as a moral-spiritual being during our last earthly life and lives before that. In this way—experiencing the plant, mineral, and animal worlds—we enter the planetary sphere. We are still engaged in the moon-sphere, but in this way we find our course into the planetary sphere. We experience the movement of the planets. We have stepped out into the cosmos along the courses of the plant-being. We are carried by the ideas of the minerals, particularly the being of the metals. We feel that a particular species of plant on the earth is an earthly reflection of what leads us to, say, Jupiter, along a spiral course that widens out more and more. But the fact that we are led to Jupiter is dependent upon our experiencing in great vividness the idea of a particular metal and particular minerals of the earth.

Once we have been led along the plant paths to a planet (always taking with us the idea of the mineral element on the earth that has borne us out [into the cosmos]), once we have reached the planet in question, this idea of the minerals that has carried us and which has become increasingly vivid, now begins to *sound* in the planet. So, after death we experience ourselves being led out on the paths of the plants; we experience the inner being of the minerals in ideas that become ever more vivid. These ideas become spiritual beings. When these livingly vivid ideas arrive at a planet—the one idea at one planet, another idea at another planet—these minerals that have become beings feel as though at home. One kind of mineral feels at home in Jupiter, another kind of mineral feels at home in Mars, and so on. And what was only regarded on earth as commonplace, now, having arrived at the planet in question, begins to sound and ring out in the most varied ways. So whereas on earth we only had these mineral reflections as something we *saw* with our senses, we now *hear* them sounding forth from the interior of the planets, and in this way we find our way into the harmony of the spheres. For in the cosmos everything is inwardly connected. What here below grows out of the earth as the plant world is the reflection of what unites the earth with the planetary system as though along paths of the plants. The mineral in the ground is actually an unassuming reflection of the force that pulls upwards along the plant paths, but which has its home out there in the planets, and represents cosmic tones in the planets which unite with each other into a great cosmic harmony.

And it is a reality when we understand what is here on earth and say of gold: in gold that glitters with its unique colour, I see the reflection of what causes a central cosmic tone to sound for my soul in the sun once I have carried [the idea of gold] up to the sun along certain courses of the plants.

When human beings have passed through this, when the necessary things I have been describing over the past few days have taken place, it then becomes possible for them to rise beyond the planetary sphere and enter the sphere of the fixed stars. They can only do this by wrenching themselves away from the moon-sphere. In a certain sense the moon-sphere has to remain behind. But what they experience in the planetary sphere as described, what they experience as the meaning of the mineral and metallic kingdom of the physical earth, what they experience as the guiding paths of the earth's plant world, all the great things they go through—this is darkened in a certain way by influences from the moon-sphere. It is darkened for them in a certain way in that they experience the elementary beings of the animal kingdom which, alongside the fully harmonious vertical up-and-down movements in which they move, also have horizontal movements. In these horizontal movements carried out by the animal group-souls within the moon-sphere, all manner of terrible archetypes for disharmonious, discrepant forces are acted out in the animal kingdom. Terrible wild battles take place between the group-souls of the animal kingdom. Through this impact of the moon sphere into the planetary sphere, what is otherwise experienced in inner calm and in a dignified and majestic way due to the archetypal nature of the plant and mineral kingdoms, gets disturbed in a certain way.

Once human beings have wrested themselves away from the moon-sphere, a cosmic memory, as we may call it, remains for them of these stupendous majestic experiences of the planetary sphere with its archetypal aspect of the mineral and plant kingdoms of the earth. This remains with them as a memory. And they enter into a world of spiritual beings whose physical and sense-perceptible reflections, as I mentioned, are the constellations. They are the constellations which, if we understand them in the right way, are the expression, the script, as it were, by which we can experience the unique qualities, the deeds and will-intentions, of the spiritual beings in the stellar sphere. We 'see' in a certain way spiritual beings who do not walk in physical bodies on the earth, but who can only be experienced in this sphere of stars. And we enter this sphere in order to imbue our being with cosmic consciousness. This cosmic consciousness has now expanded; its spatial perception has changed into a qualitative perception; its temporal perception has changed into simultaneity. [We enter this sphere] to imbue our own being with the deeds of these divine-spiritual beings.

Whereas here on earth we are enclosed in our skin, and other people in their skin do whatever they have to do, whereas here on earth we are all juxtaposed, in this starry sphere we as human souls are not only *in* one another, but our cosmic consciousness expands and we feel the world of divine-spiritual beings in ourselves as well. Here on earth we say 'we' to ourselves, or rather we each say 'I' to ourself. When we say 'I' out there, what we mean is: what I experience within my I is the world of the divine-spiritual hierarchies; I experience them as the content of my own cosmic consciousness. This of course is a still more stupendous, more expanded, more content-rich, and more majestic world of experience that we now enter. And when we become aware what forces are playing into our soul from the most diverse beings of the divine-spiritual hierarchies, we realize that these are forces which act together and have cosmic intentions all aimed towards a point. With our own soul-spiritual activity we become woven into these intentions of the divine-spiritual hierarchies and the individual beings within them. And everything we are woven into, into which is transferred our own cosmic activity, felt in our own interior, encompassed by cosmic consciousness—all this is aimed towards constructing the spirit-seed, as I described, of the human physical organism.

A saying in the ancient mysteries was indeed profound: that the human being is the temple of the gods. What is initially structured out of the spirit-cosmos in stupendous, majestic greatness, and then contracts into the human physical body to become so transformed that we no longer recognize that this archetype, this mighty majestic archetype, is actually shaped by the interrelationships of the divine-spiritual hierarchies, a work which gives these interrelationships their goal.

This sphere of experience is such that, whereas while on earth we view it from an inner standpoint centred in a point from which we look outwards in all directions, we now view this sphere from outside. For when we enter the starry sphere, already the moment we tear ourselves away from the moon-sphere, we feel we are out there in the universe and actually looking at the cosmos from outside.

I can illustrate what happens in a diagram [see diagram—*rot* = red; *blau* = blue; *gelb* = yellow]. Assume this here is the earth. It is naturally not drawn to scale, but you will understand what is meant. We look out into the expanse of the cosmos. We see the movements of the planets, and have the fixed stars out there. Our consciousness is here on the earth as though contracted into a small point [red]. We look out at the universe from a central point. The moment we escape from the moon-sphere we enter with our consciousness into the sphere of stars. But we only transit this starry sphere, as it were, led by the memory we have retained of our experiences in the planetary sphere, and [then we] enter into the sphere beyond the stars.

In this sphere beyond the stars, space actually ceases to exist. Of course, in illustrating this I have to draw spatially something that is actually [principally] qualitative. So I can draw it like this: while on earth, our consciousness is contracted as our I into this point [red—centre], when it reaches beyond the starry sphere it is peripheral [blue]. From every point we are looking inwards [blue arrows]. In this spatial diagram this way of perceiving is of course represented pictorially. If we have the constellation of Aries here [red, above left], and from our perspective on the earth we see the sun [yellow] in front of Aries, so that the sun is covering Aries, as it were, and then we arrive in the universe, we then see Aries in front of the sun.

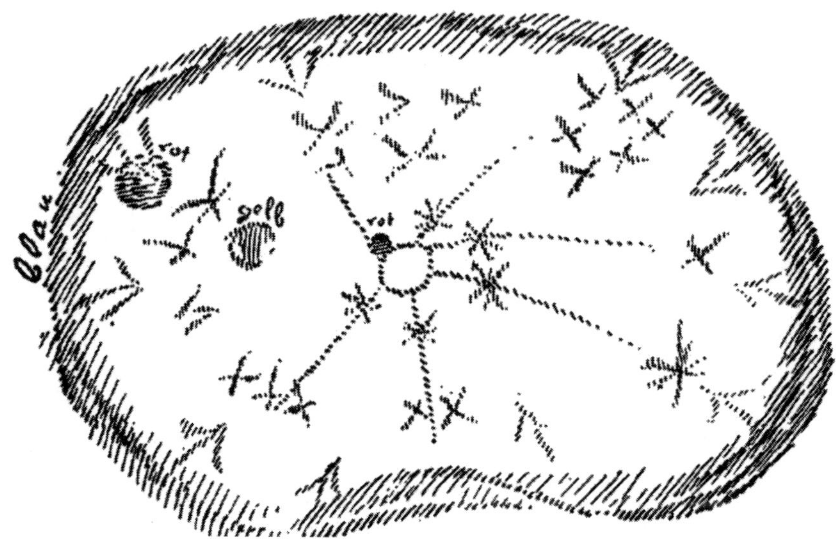

But being aware of perceiving with cosmic consciousness that Aries is in front of the sun means something different from seeing the sun in front of Aries with earthly consciousness. So in this way [from beyond the stars] we see everything spiritually. We look at the universe from outside.

And in the work of elaborating the spirit-seed of our physical organism, we actually have the forces of divine-spiritual beings in us, but such that we basically feel ourselves outside the whole cosmos that we experience on earth. And in our cosmic consciousness we now experience that we exist together with divine-spiritual beings.

When we then look back and see the constellations—but *qualitatively*, not spatially—in front of the sun, one constellation at one time and another at another time, we recognize in what we experience there and which we connect with our memory of how, after we had passed along the paths of the plants, the metals and minerals had sounded in the planets—we recognize and experience here how this sounding that was initially a cosmic music is translated into cosmic speech, into the Logos. We are able to read the intentions of the divine-spiritual beings among whom we find ourselves by experiencing the signs of this cosmic script—Aries in front of the sun, Taurus in front of the sun, and so on—by experiencing how this comes about, and how the notes that were sounded in the planets by the metals contribute sonically to this script. This instructs us on how to work on the spirit-seed of our physical organism on earth.

All the time we are in the moon sphere we have a vividly living feeling of the 'photograph' of our earthly life from a moral-spiritual perspective. We have a living feeling of what is going on down there among the animal group-souls. But these are beings of a demonic, elemental nature. Now that we find the zodiac on the far side of the sun, as it were, we learn to recognize what we actually saw there. For, this memory of animal forms, of these group-soul forms of the animals, also remains with us even on the far side of the starry sphere, and we discover that these animal group-souls—when put in terms of human language—are reflections, transformed into caricatures, of the sublime forms that now imbue our cosmic consciousness on the other side of the starry sphere as the beings of the divine-spiritual hierarchies.

So we have the beings of the divine-spiritual hierarchies beyond the starry sphere, and within the starry sphere, to the extent that it is permeated by what belongs to the moon sphere, we have the caricatures of divine-spiritual beings in the group-souls of the animals. Don't take it in an inferior sense when I say caricatures. What is a caricature from a human, humorous, artistic perspective is naturally something extremely trivial in comparison to the sublime caricature-nature of the divine-spiritual beings in the world of the moon sphere which at the same time is the world of the group-soul beings of the earth's animal kingdom. We owe an exceptional amount to the experience we have in this sphere. I spoke about this a few days ago in a form more of ideas; [2] now I'll express it in a more imaginative form.

Imagine the human being abiding up here [see illustration 2, page 10, red]. So he is looking down. He has his own proper region in the perceptions of his soul-spiritual world beyond the sphere of the stars. This is the field of his present activity. Just as when one stands on a high mountain and has sunshine above and mist below, so in this cosmic experience one has below one the whole heaving, battling group-soul condition of the animals that is in a state of rising and falling discrepancy and disharmony, but also of harmony. Like a mist of multiple shapes, it propagates this down below, expresses it there below. And, while gazing at the constellations, we see the intentions of the divine-spiritual beings, while we read there what intentions the divine-spiritual beings have, while in cosmic consciousness we learn to understand how actually this temple of the gods, this spirit-seed of the physical body, has its mysteries, those mysteries that correspond to the existence of the pure world beyond the earth and beyond the moon—we [also] look down and see what is happening there in the spiritual element of the zodiacal sphere. And, as though looking down from a sun-bathed mountain summit onto cloudy masses of mist below, we have an experience that we encapsulate in this cosmic thought: If, when you go down again, you do not take with you from this divine-spiritual world all the strength with which you have permeated yourself, you will not come through the cloudy mist-world of the animal group-souls unscathed. You will find there an image of your previous lives on earth from a moral-spiritual perspective. This will be swimming down there in the mist. You will have to pick it up once more. But all the group-souls of the animals will be there, savagely lunging at one another. All the wild commotion will be there. You will have to take powers with you from your position beyond the starry sphere that are so strong that they enable you as much as possible to keep these forces of the animal group-soul element away from your destiny. Otherwise, just as matter gathers on a crystal, what these animal group-souls cosmically sweat out according to your moral-spiritual inner core, will attach itself to you. And you will have to take with you everything you are not able to hold back by means of the forces you gathered [beyond the starry sphere], and you will have to incorporate this into yourself as all sorts of drives and instincts in your next life.

To be sure, we will only be able to extract the forces from beyond the sphere of stars if we have made ourselves capable of this extraction by having developed in ourselves a leaning towards Christ, a leaning towards the Mystery of Golgotha, to permeating our soul not in an egotistical religious way but in a truly religious way in the sense of the words of St Paul: 'Not I but Christ in me.' [3] Beyond the sphere of the stars and as we live with divine-spiritual beings, this gives us strength to permeate ourselves with forces. Then, as we descend through the moon sphere, these forces hold back from the kernel of destiny we must take with us, those forces which crowd around us in the disharmonious and discrepant interplay of the animal spiritual world that surrounds us and penetrates into the core of our soul-spiritual being.

If we want to describe what the human soul experiences between birth and death, what it unites itself with, what it absorbs in its thoughts, feelings, and will-impulses, we have to describe the earthly world surrounding us. But if we wish to describe what human beings experience between death and a new birth, we have to describe the archetypes of the things we find on earth. If we want to know what minerals really are, we must hear their being sounding forth from the planets in our life between death and a new birth. If we want to know what plants really are, then on the pathways that rise from the plant kingdom into cosmic space and are copied in the forms and structures of the plants, we must study the nature of what grows out of the soil in the plant as a faint imitation of this. If we want to study the earth's animal kingdom, we must acquaint ourselves with what is happening in the upheavals and churning of the animal group-souls in the moon sphere. And only once we have wrested ourselves away from all that, only once we have entered the sphere beyond the world of stars, do we then learn to recognize the actual mysteries of the human being. And we learn to look back on everything we experienced in the worlds of the mineral, plant, and animal archetypes.

We carry this out into the region of the cosmos in which we not only recognize the mysteries of the human being but also experience them as a living perception and are active in shaping them. Like a cosmic memory, we bring into this region everything we experienced with regard to the minerals, plants, and animals during our ascent. In the flowing-together of these memories and what we gaze on as the mysteries of human existence, what we actively experience, what we actively co-operate on—in the flowing-together of this memory and this activity, a rich and varied life is played out. And this many-sided life is what the human being undergoes between death and a new birth.

Lecture 2

DORNACH, 17 SEPTEMBER 1922

TODAY I should like to continue yesterday's discussion by bringing it even closer to human beings themselves. As you can well imagine, what one tries to bring in a presentation of this kind is inwardly so rich and varied that any presentation like the one yesterday, which covers such a broad sweep of subject matter, can only look at the subject from a single point of view, and that we can only get a feeling for what is really intended in such a presentation by means of descriptions from many different sides.

When we look at the human head, we must clearly realize that this head-formation does not only involve the head we see externally with its boundary below at the neck, but also the processes, the inner processes of organs, taking place in the human head. As 'head-processes' they are predominantly in the head, but they extend over the whole organism. Thus the head-system is essentially to be found in the whole human being but reveals itself outwardly predominantly in the head. It is the same with the chest-system, which chiefly comprises respiration and the circulation of the blood. This system also extends into the head-system as well as into the metabolic and limb system. Although, when looking at the human being, we can speak of him in a way that keeps the various systems apart, we need to be clear how, in the human being as a whole, they play into each other.

When we look at this head-system we find that during the passage through the spiritual world between death and a new birth, the metamorphoses it demonstrates are completely different from those of the other parts of the human organism. What we actually have in the head is an image of the cosmos formed as spirit-seed by an activity such as the one I described yesterday and on the days before that.

In the human head we have an image of something universal that is contracted and filled out with material existence.

If we were able to study the human head not with a physically produced microscope but with magnifying capacities of a soul-spiritual nature, we should find the whole cosmos reproduced there in its physical, etheric, astral and I-structure. We do indeed bear this whole cosmos in ourselves, and most especially in our head-system. And what is most applicable to the head-system is that between death and a new birth, in union with higher spiritual beings of the upper hierarchies, the human being works on what finds its continued development in human heredity, what in a certain sense, once it has been brought to a particular point by the human being himself in connection with the beings of the higher hierarchies in the spiritual world, falls into the physical world and, after conception, continues its development in the maternal organism.

What we find there as head-formation has indeed arisen out of the cosmos. Through the work done on it by the human being, it finally attains an astral condition in which it comes down to earth. There it continues to exist from the period before conception to the condition of actual physical development, so that what now remains of the human being is later clothed with an etheric body, but only after it has first divested itself of the germ of the physical body at the spiritual level, and been able to connect with this spirit-seed once more, which has now become physical.

Now the fact is that while we are awake, we continue on a micro-level what we accomplished on a grand universal scale in connection with divine-spiritual beings between death and rebirth. The activity carried out here goes on behind our usual human consciousness, as it were.

I'd like to show this in a diagram. When we look at the head of a person who is functioning normally, spiritual perception shows the following: when we are awake, when while awake we receive impressions of the external world in our head, what goes on in our consciousness is everything that lives in our sense-perception. I'd like to characterize what is going on in our sense-perception by first drawing the eye [see drawing], the nose from which we get impressions of smell, the palate and mouth where sensations of taste occur. The area drawn in red is meant to stand schematically for what people experience in ordinary consciousness. But in the world of things going on in people, this is not all that is happening. You know that in a great variety of ways the brain is organized into different areas. I will indicate this in the diagram [blue-green]. What is organized and integrated in this way in the brain is actually an image of the whole universe, it is the whole universe contracted into a miniature and clothed in earthly substances. Because this brain in its I-component, in its astral and etheric components, is then clothed in physical earthly matter, the earth with its forces and constituents exercises an influence on this part of the human being.

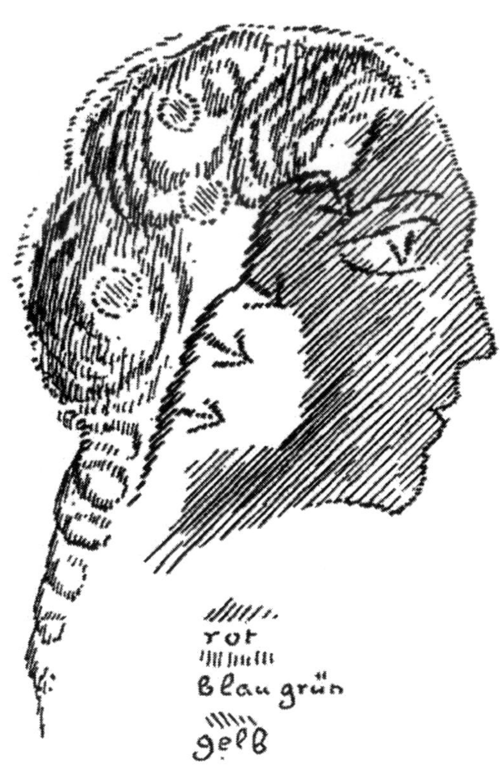

rot = red; *blau-grün* = blue-green; *gelb* = yellow

While our sense-perception is going on—while colours flow into us and are formed inside us into mental images, while sound stimuli vibrate through the human organism and, by the design of our organ of hearing, are turned into mental perceptions of hearing, while something similar is happening with our perceptions of taste, smell, and touch—while, in other words, this whole waking experience is received as the stimuli coming from the external physical sense-perceptible world, it is all living as a force in the unconscious parts of the human head-system. And while we are perceiving a colour, hearing a sound, or having a perception of taste, we are unconsciously working on creating a copy, an image of how, let's say, Jupiter stands in relation to the sun, or to Mars [yellow]. We make a copy of a cosmic relationship in our own interior. Throughout our whole waking life something is happening which we carry out behind our ordinary consciousness: the creating of images of cosmic activity. What is carried out there behind ordinary consciousness is nothing less than the lingering reverberation of what we undergo cosmically between death and a new birth or conception. We went through it there on the macro-scale of the universe. We went through it there spiritually, undeterred by earthly matter. There we did not need to extract earthly matter in subtle form, [or] wind around axes in spiralling lines and so on. There we accomplished everything in a spiritual substance. There we were accompanied in our work by the divine-spiritual powers of the highest hierarchies. What we accomplished there in association with them, we carry out here in an unconscious way by turning outwards to the sense-perceptions in our brain, by reflecting in an earthly way with earthly substances what we accomplished in a spiritual way out there [in the cosmos] with spiritual beings. In this activity we bring our pre-earthly life into our earthly life, right into the functioning of our body.

What we see in colours, hear in sounds, smell in scents, is there for us during our earth existence. What is going on in the background are thoughts that have an etheric liveliness, that only have their physical expression in the material substance of the brain. The essential thing is what is weaving etherically in the most subtle matter in the brain. Living thoughts are weaving there. Our thoughts are only reflected images that are formed using this inner cosmos where what we receive from outside rays back, and then we become conscious of it. But behind the level of memory, what I have just described is going on. There doesn't need to be anything going on behind an ordinary mirror, but behind the mirror that by means of the brain reflects back our abstract thoughts for our consciousness, an entire cosmic existence is reflected in miniature in every human being. And these living thoughts produced by us are the same for the third hierarchy—for the hierarchy of the angeloi, archangeloi and archai—as our abstractly reflecting thoughts are for us. Behind our consciousness the third hierarchy unfolds its activity through the condition of our humanness. There the beings of the archai, archangeloi, and angeloi do what has to be done and can only be done because humanity has been placed into the cosmos and on the earth. In the structuring of our brain we do not only create a mirror reflecting abstract ideas in our ordinary earthly consciousness, but something takes place in our heads which the hierarchy of angeloi, archangeloi, and archai have to accomplish on earth and through earth existence. This is a process that is just as much a part of earthly existence as any other.

We can characterize earthly life by saying that one thing or another happens through minerals; through plants there is blossoming and the bearing of fruits; something else happens through animals. What happens through human beings is that the angeloi, archangeloi, and archai pour out their activity into the spiritual atmosphere of the earth. This happens however via the subconscious activity of the human head-system.

But there is more to earthly existence than plants flowering and animals roaming: earthly existence extends beyond this into a spiritual existence. Above and beyond the plants, above the animals, above human beings, there is an activity of the angelic world, of the spiritual world, of the third hierarchy, and this activity is possible due to the human head.

Yesterday we discussed how above the plant growing out of the earth [see illustration 2, green and pink], there is an astral element.

gelb = yellow; *rosa* = pink; *grün* = green

Above the plant we have an astral configuration, a spiritual element that is higher than the blossom itself [yellow]. Likewise the activity in the human head extends further, into the spiritual, and when we look to see where it extends to, we find the activity of the beings of the third hierarchy in their association with earthly existence.

But this activity has another, very profound, significance in cosmic evolution. Behind human beings' own weaving on the earth, behind what human beings have to do in the functioning of their own organs without being aware of it, the beings of the third hierarchy are their helpers. In earthly existence, people die. We have looked at dying and tried to understand it. What dying is for human beings is for the beings of the third hierarchy a diving down into human nature. If they only had this submersion into human nature, their consciousness would fade; they would lose their essential nature. In a certain sense, they have to nourish their essential nature again and again. Nourishment from cosmic substance has to be given to the essential nature of these creatures of the third hierarchy.

Now, what is woven behind human consciousness, as I said, are predominantly formations of an etheric nature. Even during our earthly existence the boundary between internal human ether and external cosmic ether is not so sharply defined as to prevent what is set in motion in human thoughts, as human work in the brain behind conscious thoughts, from constantly vibrating out into the cosmic ether. All around their heads people are actually continuously surrounded by vibrations that are propagated out into the cosmic ether by the head activity carried out in association with the beings of the third hierarchy. And when a person passes through the portal of death, things are as I described yesterday: head activity is the first thing to fall away, and this also applies to its etheric element. But this means in reality that what happens in the head in the unconscious is the first thing to disperse into the cosmic ether and does so more rapidly. Everything that is brought about in this way by the human being leads to formations that take shape in the cosmic ether, and it is from these that the beings of the third hierarchy are nourished. Thus, on the one hand, the beings of the third hierarchy are the helpers of human beings with respect to the human head-system, and on the other hand, through what goes on within this head-system, they themselves evolve further.

Because during their earthly existence human beings are woven into earthly evolution, the beings of the third hierarchy also come into connection through them with earth-existence. These beings of the third hierarchy would otherwise belong to a world from which they could have no connection with earth-existence at all. But they have to draw their spiritual nourishment from earthly existence in the way described. So the human being is involved in a cosmic activity mediated by these third-hierarchy beings. In a certain sense this cosmic activity passes through our being. Among the higher beings immediately above man, these beings of the third hierarchy are the least powerful. They could not transform what vibrates out from man into the cosmos and has to become their spiritual nourishment, if this was completely alien to their nature. The situation, therefore, is that as little as possible of what the human being is in the rest of his nature should be mixed in with the activity that arises by means of the human head-system. Our thoughts remain logical even if with regard to morality a person accumulates a great deal of evil in life. Our thoughts remain cool with regard to other people. They remain cool to the extent that they can become the nourishment we have mentioned for higher beings.

If everything we have in our emotions were also transferred into the living thoughts that go on behind our consciousness, the angels, archangels and so on would not be in a position to absorb them. This would not be a food this hierarchy could use. Whether we are a moral person or an immoral one is certainly relevant in our normally reflected thoughts. But if I now localize the matter, which I can only do in rough outline, then what goes on towards the back of our head behind ordinary consciousness is something that remains innocent, so to speak, remains untouched by our moral aberrations. These human moral aberrations only exert an influence on the cosmic ether and on cosmic astrality to the extent that the human soul-element is associated with the respiratory system, with the circulatory system of the blood. In a certain sense the head is a pure image of the cosmos. And what during our earthly life exists behind our ordinary consciousness as an image of universal cosmic activity, where worlds are continuously being formed and continuously destroying themselves, what goes on there is present with a certain purity as compared with the rest of our human nature. But it is nevertheless the case that if you could turn your eyes backwards and become spiritually sighted, and these eyes that are turned back in their sockets and have become spiritually clairvoyant could look back into the interior cavity of the cranium, they would see stars continuously lighting up, stars related to one another in movement, a world of fixed stars. A whole cosmos in miniature would become visible.

Things are different in the human chest-system from how they are in the head-system. Where breathing and blood circulation as the rhythmic aspect of our being take place, there is indeed also an image of the cosmos, but earthly conditions exert a far greater influence here. To a far greater degree they change what plays in as the image of the cosmos. If, in the functioning of our lungs, we were able to turn ourself around, as it were, and were able to see not what is clothed in earthly matter but the etheric and astral constituents of this, we would be able to see what is happening in the interior of the lung as a star, as a planet, as a world of sun and moon. But earthly conditions are constantly playing into this inner existence. Here the earth has a far greater influence. We need to bear in mind that what works into the head-system directly, and directly into the formations I have just described, is something that is just as subtle as what the eyes make of the world of colour, what is made of the world of sound through the body. This integrates itself into the cosmic activity. And what intrudes into this is what is brought about by the rest of the organism in its breathing, in the blood that is also functioning in the brain. This is intruding matter that fills out [the head-system]. But the configuration, the inner sculpture that is at work there [in the head-system], is a thorough image of the cosmos. There the earth has no influence.

The situation is completely different in the chest-system. The chest-system takes in air and changes it. This is something in our immediate earthly surroundings, something that does not enter the human organism in such a subtle way as that which the eyes make out of colour. The air we breathe is coarser than the colourful light that enters our organism. This coarser breath therefore has a far stronger, a more altering influence on everything in the chest-system that is an image of cosmic processes. And even more so when we look at the blood! All our food is involved in our blood circulation. First it is ingested as food, transformed by digestive processes, and released into the circulating blood.

When blood goes into the head, it does so in an extraordinarily rarefied condition, a condition which the intimations of ancient clairvoyance rightly called a phosphorous condition. This is an extraordinarily refined state. Here the image of cosmic activity has power over matter so that matter is unable to unfold its own forces. If a salt of some kind enters the brain and wants to develop its own forces there, it is 'drowned out', overwhelmed by the processes and activity exercised by the image of the cosmos [rather than] in the thicker blood circulation that takes place in the organs of the chest. In the chest-organs the influence coming in from the human being is far greater. The image of the cosmos there undergoes a far stronger change. Consequently, when one looks clairvoyantly at the human chest-system, it appears in the way I can roughly illustrate as follows [see drawing].

We see here how when we inhale, an image of the cosmos lights up. In the brain we really see a whole cosmos at play. For the brain this is only interrupted in our sleep-life. [In the chest] sleep-life doesn't interrupt anything, but the whole thing interrupts itself continuously. Seen with spiritual sight the chest-system shows stars, also star-movements, but distorted towards the back and becoming indistinct towards the front. The cosmos is also reflected in a certain sense in people's chest in so far as there are processes on our earth that are completely dependent on the regular course of the months in the year, according to which the plants come up and die down again. There is regularity here. We find expressed in plant forms the spiral courses I described earlier. There is a mineral tendency [in this regularity] which, to be sure, stretches out over long periods, but which in a certain way also takes place in cosmic regularity. In the air currents moving over the earth certain changes occur which

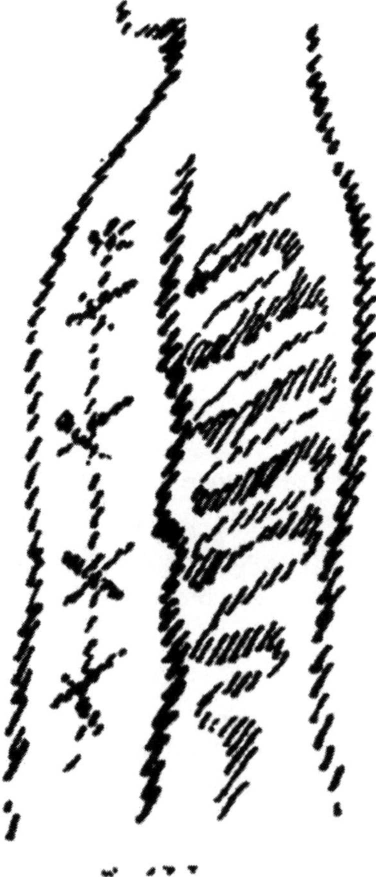

we can observe for example in the metamorphoses of the weather over the course of the year. But into this there falls the irregularity of cloud formation, the real changeability of the weather. Into this there falls the moods of meteorology. The moods of meteorology intrude into the cosmic element.

Thus in the human chest, in its connection with the back, there is a distorted cosmos. The impression this makes is as though we were to take the surrounding cosmos with us into the night, and that a giant tugged at it from one side, and another giant tugged at it from the other side, so that instead of a rounded cosmos we get an elongated barrel-shape, somewhat thicker in the middle. This is how the cosmos appears to spiritual sight towards the back; and towards the front it appears as though thrown into confusion. Just as weather conditions over the surface of the earth are ever-changing, so the cosmos towards our front appears confused. The way it works as a whole is that the cosmos is lighting up at one moment and fading away the next; it lights up when we breathe in and disappears when we breathe out. Just as the human being brings about physical processes through respiration, so inhalation causes the lighting up of the distorted cosmos and exhalation causes a darkening of the distorted cosmos once more.

The Indian yogi tried in his yoga exercises to experience this lighting up and fading away of the distorted cosmos. And he endeavoured thereby to reveal the real structure of the cosmos by permeating what he perceived in this way—through enlivening his breath to the point where it enabled him to perceive this inner distorted cosmos—with what he was then able to determine through contemplation. Thus, as chest-beings, we experience the cosmos a second time, but as though in a struggle with chaos.

And we also experience the cosmos a third time; this time in a form that actually seems completely indistinct, for that is the way it is integrated into our metabolic and limb system. In this system we can barely make out to what extent what is incorporated here astrally and in relation to the I, has emerged from the cosmos. For this reason in the lectures I have given here, I have had to call what is incorporated in this system 'embryonic', for it is actually a cosmos in a state of becoming. The situation here is that only when we move our limbs, or when our metabolism is active, does what appears as a cosmos in-the-making relate in a similar way to what it submerses itself into. When I raise my leg, the spiritual element of this third human system shoots, as it were, into the leg movement and into the inner processes that arise in association with it.

I would have to draw this third element in a diagram [see drawing] to show that there is nothing to be seen here of the cosmos that is present so distinctly in the head-system, that is present in distorted form, dampened down and obscured with respect to spiritual light, both in the respiratory system and in the limb and digestive system [red]. Everything here is actually still as though in a cosmic nebula. We can study cosmic nebulae in outer space. But with spiritual sight we can also study cosmic nebulae microscopically, in miniature, when we look at the third part of the human being, the limb and metabolic system. Here we see how this nebula structure [bluish] is in the stars [yellow] as though wanting to arise as light, but the moment it lights up it fades away again. We can see how this is completely overwhelmed by what issues from the earth. Here the chemical affinities, the chemical forces of the earth's substances play a significant role.

How the various earthly substances relate chemically to each other is far more important during earthly life than how the things relate that we bring with us from the cosmos. And yet the human being is connected to the spiritual worlds through this part [the limb and metabolic system] of his organism as well. We are related to the spiritual worlds through our chest-system because there is a spiritual hierarchy related to our chest-system just as there is a spiritual hierarchy related to our head-system. In our head it is the third hierarchy; in our chest-system it is the second hierarchy, the exusiai, dynamis, and kyriotetes. This [second] hierarchy develops a cosmic function by means of earthly human beings, by making use of what takes place in the human chest-system. And their activity is one that is far more spiritual than the activity of the third hierarchy. The third hierarchy [through its less spiritual activity] is therefore able to bear what finally leads to images in matter. In the structure

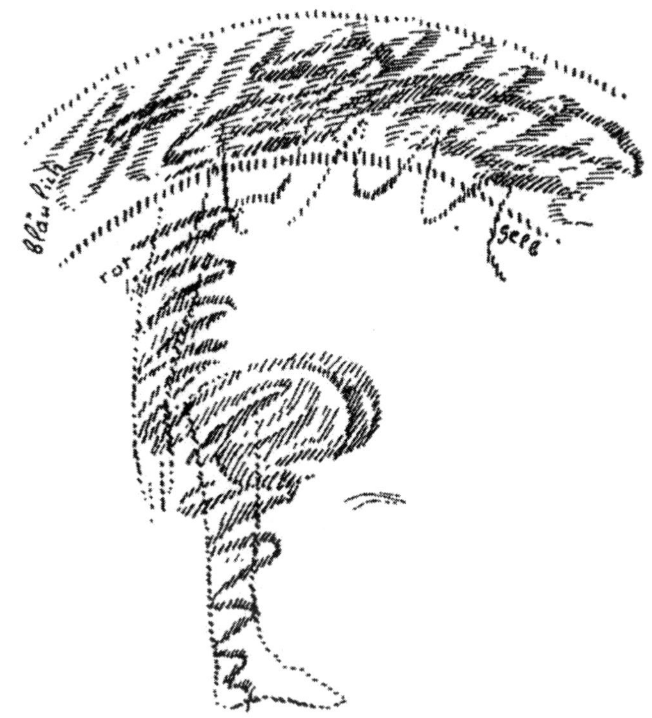

bläulich = bluish; *rot* = red; *gelb* = yellow

of the human head we therefore really have a material image of the cosmos. In the chest-system we have a distortion precisely because matter does not become a faithful image of the cosmos, because it is destroyed again and again and can also be dissolved; the cosmic formation is not finished. So we have an earthly element coming into play very strongly [in the head], and a cosmic element [in the chest-system] that is never finished in the human being, something that remains cosmic so that, in so far as we breathe and have a circulation, human beings are permeated by a cosmic activity in which there works and weaves the activity of the second hierarchy. And into this the human being inserts the living 'photograph' I spoke about yesterday and in the preceding lectures, which is an image of his moral and spiritual qualities.

By having lungs and processes in these lungs that extend further into the functioning of respiration, by having a circulation and the gently percussive strokes of this circulation that vibrate out into the cosmic ether and even into cosmic astrality, man is woven into the activity of the second hierarchy. His being itself creates cosmic effects, and the beings of the second hierarchy integrate themselves into what is brought about cosmically through him. But the longer his life is, the more man inserts into this the living image of his moral and spiritual qualities, this elemental being which, as I told you, is created by people during their lives. Every night, by the way, this elemental being emerges to some extent out of the person, and one can see the predominating activity exercised in it by the second hierarchy. When we are awake during the day [this elemental being] goes back into the person, and the waking activity continues to permeate it with the moral and spiritual values and qualities of the individual in question.

Now, what takes place in the metabolic-limb system is connected with the first hierarchy. The connection here is primarily with the seraphim, cherubim, and thrones. This is the system in which the human being is most physical, is most given up to physical forces. It is as though the cosmic element plays into it only nebulously. But into this quietly nebulous cosmic activity that is in him, which in its material functioning is permeated by strong, intensive chemical operations, by the elements of physics—[into this activity] there flames and floods and thrusts the activity of the seraphim, cherubim, and thrones. For it is they who, through their spiritual power, are able to manage the toughest material element, and it will be the beings of this hierarchy who will one day transfer the earthly processes of chemistry and physics from their earthly form into their Jupiter form, as I have described in my *Occult Science*. But this activity, which actually takes place in the cosmos, is subtly inscribed during our lifetime by what flashes through us from the will-aspect of the soul (as I have discussed in previous lectures) and in which are to be found the quiet cosmic processes that are loosely compounded with the earthly element and the processes of chemistry and physics that overwhelm the cosmic element.

Here [see diagram 2.4], in the limb and metabolic system, the earth has full possession of the human being, if I can put it like that. In this system during our earthly life the earthly outweighs the cosmic. In our chest-system the cosmic is in balance with the earthly. In the head-system the cosmic is predominant. This is why the head-system can only be connected with the lowest beings of the higher hierarchies. Where the earth predominates, the strongest spiritual beings are at work—the seraphim, cherubim, and thrones—because here man is more torn away from his being by the earth.

And when we go through the portal of death, when our physical organism falls away, that which is only a nebulous spiritual element is absorbed into the activity of the seraphim, cherubim, and thrones, and gradually woven into them. But into this activity there sinks down what had previously taken shape in our chest-system as the living image of the moral and spiritual aspect of the human being. What was previously in the stream of the middle hierarchy, if I can put it like that, now goes into the stream of the first hierarchy. It thereby gains greater intensity in the conditions of the cosmos so that, in their middle portion, human beings develop their karma as a living elemental being. This is then taken up by the stream of the first hierarchy. And while the human being is living through his life between death and a new birth, while he escapes from his karmic counter-image and ascends into the world where he can work with higher beings on the archetype of his physical organism, while the human being experiences all this, which he finds once more in this image on his return, something else is happening. During the period in which the human being leaves the soul-world and abides in spirit-land, the living image of the destiny he himself has created is transferred back from the beings of the highest hierarchy—the seraphim, cherubim, and thrones—to the second hierarchy and finally passed on to the third hierarchy—to the angeloi, archangeloi, and archai. And when the human being enters into [earthly] life once more, it [this image] is incorporated into what plays between the third hierarchy of angeloi, archangeloi, and archai, and his head-system. Everything the human being created through his earthly being and handed over to the cosmos after death; everything the human being developed because he has a material organism governed by earthly forces and which he had to give to the seraphim, cherubim, and thrones; everything he had to let stream into the cosmos in this way—this, indeed, he receives once more via the path by which the angeloi, archangeloi, and archai work through his head-system in a new life on earth. The human being gives to the seraphim, cherubim, and thrones the destiny that he himself has caused, and receives it back from the angeloi, archangeloi, and archai. They carry it into the activity that he carries out in a new life on earth. In this way, in his new earthly destiny, he receives from the third hierarchy that which he had passed on to the first hierarchy when leaving his last life.

So you see that we understand the universe as a whole only when we place the context in which our senses here can perceive and our intellect can think, into the [greater] context that reveals itself to real sight. For there it is not only growing plants that appear, not only water in cloud formations, in currents, not only physical stars—what appears there is the whole cosmos in its living potency, spiritually imbued by ranks of hierarchies that engage in what is just as much an activity as physical activity is, an activity that surges and billows through this physical activity. And events take place during our existence between death and re-birth such that our human destiny is transferred from the hands of the seraphim, cherubim, and thrones to the angeloi, archangeloi, and archai. We thereby receive what we are to experience in our new life as our destiny. What we left behind with the highest hierarchy is given back to us by the hands of the third hierarchy. And together with the third hierarchy during our earthly life, we have, through our compensatory deeds, to integrate it once more into cosmic balance.

LECTURE 3

DORNACH, 22 SEPTEMBER 1922

IN the previous lectures I tried to describe in detail the connection between the physical and soul aspects of the human being with the spiritual powers of the cosmos. Today I should like to add to that picture by describing details from a historical perspective, connections of historical life with the spiritual worlds, in a similar way to how this was done for the physical and soul-existence of the human being.

In our materialistic age the study of history is restricted to its external aspect. People simply try to describe what occurs in the physical-sensory world while giving no consideration to how the spiritual world plays into the historical actions of humanity. Our age is completely lacking in the possibility of looking at the connection between what people do during the course of history and the beings and powers that are behind human existence.

Today we'll take a look at ancient times of human development, beginning with the ages which in my book *Occult Science*[4] I have called the ancient Indian and the ancient Persian epochs. Naturally there were many different things done by people in this age that we view as the subject of history. But we need to be clear that precisely in that age the actions taking effect externally as history were facts that resulted least of all from people's consciousness; for as we know, it was precisely in those ancient times that people's consciousness was permeated and pervaded by a kind of dreamlike clairvoyance. Pictures appeared to people in their consciousness, and spiritual beings played into the content of these pictures, which stimulated people to act in certain ways.

Now, in the age we are speaking about, the process of inhalation played an extraordinarily important role in human life. You will realize, just from the fact that through yoga exercises the breathing-process in those times had become a conscious process, a process of perception, that breath played a great role in those ancient times, and principally inhalation more than exhalation. We are simply not aware in our present age that apart from the coarse substantiality we expect to find in the air when we inhale, there are all sorts of other substances there as well, but in an exceptionally subtle and rarefied form. The substances that in our present earthly existence we otherwise find in a solid mineral state are also distributed in a very rarefied way throughout the atmosphere, and people breathe these in. But these substances, in their highly rarefied distribution in the atmosphere, have the curious tendency to create forms. Certainly, matter in earthly substance also takes on form. We know these forms as mineral crystals. But these are not the crystals I mean at the moment. I mean those substances that are finely distributed in the atmosphere, we can also say in the etheric atmosphere in so far as this permeates the air. These substances also create forms, but these forms are not like the forms of the minerals; rather, they are similar to the forms of human organs. This is a peculiarity of the ether permeating the air. If we are able to observe this ether, how it permeates the air and how it can appear for imaginative cognition, we perceive in this ether subtle etheric forms flying around, as it were, which have the shape of a lung, the shape of the liver or stomach, at any rate the shapes of human inner organs. If we are trained in etheric perception, we can observe all human forms out there in the cosmic ether. But in comparison to our physical organs, these organ-forms as a rule are of gigantic size. We see huge etheric liver-forms, lung-forms pervading the space of the cosmos around us.

What is flying around out there as forms, as it were, is what people breathe in. And it is good that they can do this because, by inhaling, these forms that enter us with the air work on our organs in a restorative, health-giving way. During the course of life our organs deteriorate more and more. And in a certain sense, if I can express it somewhat crudely, they are 'patched up' by what is inhaled.

We know how difficult it is for therapies to patch up human organs. But the therapy meant here must actually work on people constantly, and indeed it does.

Now, in those most ancient times of historical human development, people were able without any particular training, by virtue of their dreamlike clairvoyance, to see these etheric forms and also their significance for the human being. They were able to see what it meant, let's say, when the human stomach-form which was dissolved in etheric pepsin-like substances was breathed in and absorbed by the stomach. People were very aware of such things in ancient times, and the further back we go, the more aware people were of their relationship with the subtle aspects of their environment.

But this process of etheric forms entering people when they inhaled,[5] was not simply automatic, was not simply a matter of people sucking air into themselves as though into an emptied air-space. It was not simply a matter of people breathing in, because in this process, in this submersion, as it were, of cosmic forms into the human being, an activity of spiritual beings was involved. Let's assume that this is one of these forms [see drawing 3.1]. The person breathes in, the form dives down into the individual [red]. But an activity of spiritual beings is involved here at the same time.

In the lectures I gave recently[6]—some public and some given here—we got to know spiritual beings of a particular kind and their significance for human beings. The beings meant here are those that have their physical image in the moon and its moonlight; they are the spiritual moon-beings. In the times I have been speaking about, it was these spiritual moon-beings who were able to shape their way from the outer cosmic circle into the human being by means of these forms. So, in their process of inhalation in those ancient times of human development on earth, people breathed the spiritual moon-cosmos into themselves and stimulated the moon-beings to a particular activity in themselves.

What I have just related was the content of a science and wisdom much studied in the most ancient mystery schools of humanity. For, the initiates of these mystery schools knew that human beings were subject to these processes, that they drew the spiritual moon-cosmos into themselves. But they also knew that this drawing-in took place predominantly at night when people were asleep. But because all people in primal times had a dreamlike clairvoyance, an intermediary state between waking and sleeping, one could count on these spiritual moon-beings being drawn into people also during certain times of the day. And the whole guidance the initiates of the ancient mysteries carried out for humanity relied on controlling what these moon-beings brought into human beings by way of the process of inhalation. This enabled people to utilize in their own activity the forces of these moon-beings who had made their way into human beings by this path.

You need to realize that today's intellectual mode of teaching did not exist in those ancient times. Nevertheless the initiates had ways and means of guiding and leading the populace in a far more intensive way than was the case later on or indeed is the case today. For example, in the most ancient times of human development, the skill was most definitely developed in the mysteries of speaking with the moon-beings that were breathed in by people during the night and during the active intermediary periods of clairvoyance in the day. The initiates spoke to these beings in the mysteries and stimulated them to bring very specific things into humanity. This was the magnificent means by which the initiates of the ancient mysteries were able to lead the people, and whereby the moon-beings were their helpers via the process of inhalation. Humanity today has very inadequate ideas about the particular and extraordinarily mysterious processes that were outwardly reflected in all manner of rituals and ceremonies performed in ancient times in order for the mystery centres to lead humanity.

But a different age arose with humanity's advancing development. The old clairvoyance faded away more and more so that those special procedures that could be performed by the initiates of the original Indian and original Persian periods, as I have just described, became increasingly difficult. To be sure, in certain regions, remnants of the old clairvoyance lasted up to the Mystery of Golgotha and even a few centuries beyond. But it was very dim, and already in the third and second millennia before the Mystery of Golgotha the procedures I have just described were no longer performed with the same intensity as in the very ancient times of human development immediately after the age of Atlantis. We could say that the initiates of the mysteries found themselves increasingly at a loss when they wanted to use the force of the moon-beings in order to lead humanity. To explain what was going on between the initiates of the mysteries and the moon-beings that were used in ancient times in the procedures I have described, I should like to express it like this: when, for example, an initiate already of the Egypto-Chaldean period approached a moon-being and wanted to give him a task that involved the moon-being entering [the human being] through inhalation and imprinting certain things into the human soul, the moon-being responded, as it were, by saying to the initiate: 'During the day, we no longer have shelter on earth, we can only find shelter during the night.' But it would have seemed highly dubious to the initiate to work on people via the moon-beings during the night, because this would be treating people in an automatic way, as it were. Something would have come about which, to use a certain terminology, one would definitely call black magic. The good initiates naturally kept far away from this. So it was of tremendous significance for them when the moon-beings, who were supposed to be their helpers in their guidance of humanity, answered them by saying: 'During the day we have no shelter on earth.' Thus the initiates of these mysteries faced the danger of having no helpers on the paths they had used for guiding humanity.

What came later on the other hand, through the Mystery of Golgotha, had also not yet arrived. Thus there was an intermediary period between the very ancient age of clairvoyance, in which everything I have described could take place, and the age ushered in by the Mystery of Golgotha when all working of the spirit on earth was changed. We can study this intermediary period most particularly in the culture of ancient Egypt.

Egyptian development followed on from the ancient Persian period. The initiates of Chaldean humanity did not know what to do with respect to the question I have just mentioned. In a certain sense they were completely baffled by it and consequently took a rather external route to look for what they needed to guide humanity: [they turned to] their star wisdom, to their art of interpreting the stars. What the Chaldean initiates learnt through their astrology was what in those more ancient times could be learnt through the moon-beings who entered people via inhalation. Now however, these beings said they could find no shelter on the earth. And so people substituted the force that was previously given inwardly, as it were, with the force of external observation.

The initiates of the Egyptian world sought to deal with the problem in a completely different way. The Egyptian initiates looked for ways and means to provide the moon-beings with shelter on the earth. So the Egyptian initiates now tried to create this shelter for the beings who, according to the primal and eternal laws of world evolution, were no longer destined to have shelter on earth. And it was precisely the mystery-priests of Egypt who found a means of providing shelter for the moon-beings of luciferic form.

This puzzle of how to get the moon-spirits to descend once more to earth even though, according to the eternal evolution of the world, they were no longer destined to do so, was solved by the Egyptian priests by populating their burial sites with mummies. I have mentioned this in previous lectures from another perspective.[7] I would like to mention it today from this cosmic-historical perspective.

The mummified corpse of the human being became the shelter for the luciferically configured moon-gods. In ancient times something could be observed in a natural way by simply coming together with people and clairvoyantly observing their breathing. This no longer took place in these natural processes but, through the old inhalation, it had swarmed around, as it were, in societal life, and played a role in humanity. This was now substituted in the sites where the spirits that found no shelter in humanity during the day—spirits that would have had to wander the earth without shelter, and could not have been used for the events of earthly history—were accommodated, as it were, in mummified human bodies. Mummies were the habitation of the moon-beings. And when an Egyptian initiate stood with full understanding before a mummy, he studied by means of this mummy what had previously been studied outside in the freshness of life. He observed what the moon-gods were carrying out in these habitations provided for them. And in this way the initiates became aware of what they could inculcate into human historical development in the most manifold ways.

As paradoxical as it may seem to the materialistically-minded person of today, it is nevertheless true that if we want to understand what took place historically in the development of the Egyptian cultural epoch, there is no other way than by studying not merely the external historical monuments but by studying in the eternal cosmic chronicle through imaginative and inspiritive sight what is to be read there about the activity of the spiritual moon-entities for whom no external monuments have been erected, and who have left behind no historical documents. But the actions of the people who did erect external monuments was inspired by the spiritual moon-beings via an indirect route. [It was inspired] through the work of initiates with the moon-beings once shelter had been provided for these beings in mummies during daytime on earth. And we only learn to recognize properly the origin of what is to be found in the written documents if we can find the beings in the cosmic chronicle that say to us: During the period of the third, second, first pre-Christian millennia, we could only inhabit the earth because the Egyptian initiates gave us earthly habitations in mummies. We can learn from these moon-beings the source of the intentions behind the historical actions of that time.

If we wish to know man in his true being, we must go to the stars and the hierarchies, as I discussed in the previous two lectures. But if we wish to know humanity's historical development in the right way, we have to be able to study the spiritual powers that play into this historical development. Thus we have to be prepared to study the significance of such a striking phenomenon as mummification in ancient Egypt. When we are really able to do research using spiritual science, we learn to see the inner meaning of things which, for people with today's materialistic perceptions, appear merely as a strange custom. Mummies were once habitations of gods. Moon-beings that had become luciferic had their habitation in mummies.

In the fourth post-Atlantean epoch, in the Greek and Roman period, things became somewhat different. The dominance of inhalation ceased. Inhalation was still significant, but its dominant quality came to an end. And inhalation and exhalation became processes of equal importance for humanity. This is something to which the Greek initiates paid special attention in their work. And that wonderful state of balance between inhalation and exhalation which was a special feature of the Greeks, enabled Greek art in its exemplary nature to emerge in history in the way it did.

The Greeks were not particularly predisposed to absorb the moon-beings by inhalation. Through their initiates, what was typical of the Greeks was to bring into operation those beings that developed a quality of half flying, half swimming in the air, and that liked most to rock themselves in the state of balance between inhalation and exhalation. And when we go back into those ancient times of Greek development when the actual inspiration for what was to emerge later in a more external form was first given; when we go back to the times that give us the origins of the sublime primitive forms from which Greek sculpture, Greek tragedy, and Greek philosophy emerged—we find that the initiates in particular of the Greek mysteries were gifted most especially in using those beings for their guidance of humanity that rocked themselves gently in the balance brought about between human inhalation and exhalation.

And fundamentally speaking, we cannot learn the art of Apollo and the Orphic wisdom without recognizing that each of these received their special soul quality because their helpers were elemental-demonic beings that moved on this equilibrium of inhalation and exhalation. The tuning of the strings of Apollo's lyre was derived from what one could observe when the beings danced upon the balance between human in-breath and out-breath, between the moon-sphere and the earth-sphere, danced, we could say, on the strings of the cosmos that were woven in equilibrium through inhalation and exhalation. What was imitated in the tuning of the strings on the lyre of Apollo and other similar things, were the dances of the air-demons. If we wish to ascertain what happened historically in the external world, we have to look into the spiritual world.

Recall what I said here not so long ago: that chanting, the development of recitative, the development of the hexameter, is based on the ratio in our rhythmic aspect between the rhythm of respiration and the rhythm of blood circulation. Recall what I discussed in this regard in the course given over in the other building [8] relating to the structure of the hexameter. The study required to discover the hexameter was once a very concrete study for Greek initiates.

When we breathe in, we take in the vibrations of the cosmos and adapt them to our inner being. When we breathe out we impart to our breath-rhythm something of the vibrating pulse in our blood circulation. Thus we can say that, in our inhalation, the outer world pulsates into us, and in our exhalation the pulsing of our own blood lives outwards. Thus the Greek initiates, who were trained in this matter, could observe around people in their etheric and astral bodies how cosmic rhythm and pulse rhythm met, how they wafted and mingled together, and how upon [these rhythms] the air-demons rocked themselves and carried out their dances. This is the study Homer [9] was called upon to undertake when he developed the hexameter to its full blossoming, for it is born out of the relationship of the human being to the cosmos.

Many historical things only become clear when we look at them with the eye of one who understands art, with a discerning artistic eye. I will not go into the fact that the materialistic thinking of our time, instead of actually pondering the special way in which the Homeric verses came about, assists itself by saying that a Homer did not exist at all. That is by far the simplest thing to do from the standpoint of the current materialistic mindset. Comprehending Homer is something that is impossible for materialistic knowledge. And what one cannot comprehend is not permitted to exist according to the way of thinking that in our time has become so proud and vain. What cannot be understood by the academic intellect ought not to exist and doesn't exist. People can't understand Homer, so therefore there was no Homer. But maybe something else would be better!

In museums everywhere we can still find sculptures of the head of Homer. Now, I'm not saying that this Homer head is particularly good, but it is good enough that when we look at this Homer who is portrayed as blind, and who despite his blindness has a very special expression in his eyes and holds his head in a curious way, when we enter into this position of the head we get the feeling that he was blinded voluntarily—I'm speaking figuratively—so that seeing would not disturb him in a profound listening. He listens to what he perceives in the pulses vibrating together in the pulse of the cosmos and the pulse of human blood, of the human etheric body, and on which the air-beings perform their harmonious and melodious dances. What he hears there is a different kind of whirring sound, like when we listen to the whirring of a swarm of gnats, where there is a whirring of the hexameter; what he hears in this whirring, while he is undisturbed by sight or ordinary bright daylight, condenses for him in such a way that his ears also become organs of touch, as it were.

Look at a sculpted head of Homer with this in mind! There is a touching hearing, a hearing touching, there is a very special kind of life that moves through this plaster or marble form. Something is partially released in this head-nature that flashes from inside through the blind eyes, something that doesn't only hear but touches the tones and takes hold of the tactile tone in order to transpose it into the chanting organ of the voice, something that was taken into the human being from the cosmos at a time when neither inhalation on the one hand nor exhalation on the other predominated, but when an intermingled sounding of both existed, the in-breath and the out-breath.

The question that someone looking at the head of Homer should be most curious to ask is: How does he breathe? This head is completely undistracted by external light. It is fully devoted to the mysteries of the breath. This feeling about the Homer sculpture which can be seen everywhere, would make more sense than trying to argue ancient Homer away.[10] The arguments for dismissing Homer were so tempting and beguiling that even Goethe[11] did not deal with them fully.

The first person during Goethe's time to argue Homer away, to say that Homer had not existed at all, was the German philologist Wolf.[12] But even Goethe could not escape the tempting and alluring arguments of this philologist. And although he always felt a horror at the idea that Wolf had devoured Homer, on the other hand he was also partly confounded by the immensely clever arguments that were propounded. Just look at all the things modern cleverness can do! People have really become extraordinarily clever. But being clever doesn't necessarily mean knowing anything about the world.

Herman Grimm[13] later attempted—not to bring Homer back to life, to be sure, since Wolf had not devoured Homer but only a perception of Homer that had emerged over time—Herman Grimm later attempted the following. He said, let us not concern ourselves initially about Homer, let us not concern ourselves about Wolf who has devoured him, but look at Homer's *Iliad* itself. Let us try to read this Homeric epic not in the way a philologist reads it but how an ordinary person reads it. Let us take Book I and see what artistic quality was used in composing it. Then let us look at how it continues, how it develops. Let us go to the next book, to Book II. Curious: we find again and again how each book is developed with an inner composition, as though with a wonderful artistic feeling, that is similar to the previous book.

Taking this approach, Herman Grimm goes through the whole *Iliad*. And he says: If Homer never existed, it would be highly curious if over the course of time first one portion of the *Iliad*, then a second, then a third were composed and then all collected together.

In this way philologists might come to the view that *Faust* was also composed like this because one could find inconsistencies in it. At any rate it would be a very strange circumstance if such an inwardly coherent composition as the *Iliad* had been put together from all sorts of fragments from different places.

It is necessary to go so deeply into history that we bear in mind the weaving and working of spiritual beings into the direct processes of history. This is something anthroposophical spiritual science must also endeavour to do, and I have tried to realize this for you today with regard initially to more ancient times up to Greek culture. Tomorrow we will see how in our present history since the Mystery of Golgotha, these spiritual beings still show themselves to be active in human actions although these actions are becoming freer and freer. And we will see how to find what we ourselves need to do; whether perhaps we need to help ourselves much as the Egyptian initiates did when they provided shelter for certain moon-beings. Perhaps our own times require, based on a proper spirit-knowledge, that something similar must gain ground.

Lecture 4

DORNACH, 23 SEPTEMBER 1922

In our considerations of the human being, I spoke yesterday about matters to do with history in so far as these lead us into the spiritual world, and I looked at two earlier epochs of human development from that perspective. I drew attention to how the more ancient initiates endeavoured to guide the people in religious, social, and other matters, by selecting as their helpers those spiritual beings that are connected with human breathing. And we saw how these beings in turn are connected in the cosmos with what reveals itself outwardly as moonlight. We can therefore speak about certain moon-beings being used as helpers during the period when such things were necessary (namely in the Egyptian period) to give direction to the religious and social life of ancient Egypt and to other areas besides in that ancient historical development.

We then saw the importance of certain beings in Greek culture which yesterday I called elemental luciferic beings. These were used as helpers by the Greek initiates, for example those in the Orphic mysteries, to inaugurate Greek art. I pointed out how even today, if we have a somewhat deeper and more intimate sensitivity for such things, we can see in the traditional sculpture of Homer's head the profound listening of this human individual to what yesterday I called a touching hearing, a hearing touching, and what was essentially a listening to spiritual beings. These were the air-beings that used the state of balance between human inhalation and exhalation in order to establish a rhythm between respiration and blood circulation. Through the wonderful ratio that existed in human beings between breath-rhythm and pulse-rhythm, the Greek hexameter could arise, and indeed all the other Greek meters. These were a creation both of the human being and of the rhythm, so full of mystery, that undulates and vibrates through the entire cosmos. I said that when the Greeks speak of Apollo's lyre, we can think how the strings of this lyre were tuned according to impressions attained from the perception of this combined rhythm.

Since that time humankind has entered upon a completely different development, and I have drawn attention on many occasions to the characteristic features of this development from the most varied points of view. I have drawn attention to the fact that ever since the fifteenth century, humanity has been in the grip of the intellectual element that dominates all human culture and civilization today in the broadest sense. It arose in modern development because an older language, which in its primary form was connected with what I called that deep listening to rhythm in the Greco-Latin period, because the Latin language continued deep into the Middle Ages and completely intellectualized itself. So that in many respects the educating of modern humanity into modern intellectualism has been brought about by the Latin language.

This intellectualism that is based on thoughts completely dependent on the development of the physical body, is actually bringing the whole of humanity into the danger of falling away from the spiritual world. And indeed we can say that if the old religions speak of a more ancient form of fall, seen more as a moral fall, then we must speak of the danger for modern humanity as being that of an intellectual fall.

The general thoughts of humanity today, which people regard as having the greatest authority, the so-called clever thoughts of modern science—these intellectual structures are founded entirely on the human physical body. We mustn't believe that, when a modern person thinks, he is assisted in this by anything other than the physical body. Thoughts in earlier ages were something completely different. In earlier periods of historical development thoughts came to people along with certain spiritual visual perceptions. Visual perceptions either pressed through to people from the cosmos, or could also rise up out of their inner being. We could say that thoughts were carried on the waves of these spiritual perceptions. These were thoughts spiritually given, thoughts that were sent to people from the spiritual world, thoughts that revealed themselves to humanity. Intellectualism has no access to thoughts such as these.

When we ourselves form our thoughts purely following logic, which is what modern people strive to do, our consciousness is thereby bound to our physical body. It is not that thoughts themselves arise from this physical body; that is naturally not the case at all. But the forces that are active in these thoughts are not in modern people's awareness. They don't get to know thoughts in their true nature. All the thoughts that modern people already receive at school, what they absorb as popular science, what is to be found in popular literature: all these thoughts in their actual substance, in what lives in them, are unknown to the modern person. They know them only as reflections. The physical body is the mirror, and people are not aware of what is actually living in their thoughts; they are aware only of what the physical body reflects back to them of these thoughts. For if people could really live into these thoughts, they would be able to perceive their [own] pre-earthly existence. They are unable to do this. Modern people cannot perceive pre-earthly existence because they do not live in the substance of their thoughts, only in thought-reflections. These thoughts are not realities.

And this is what is so dangerous for modern humanity: that in these thoughts there is spirit as very substance, there is pre-earthly life, but people know nothing of this; they only know the reflections. Due to this, something that is actually meant for the spiritual world (for, these thoughts are indeed meant for the spiritual world, they are rooted in the spiritual world) falls away from the spiritual world in modern humanity and is reflected by the physical body. And what is reflected there is only the external sense-world. So we might really speak of a fall for modern times that is evident in the sphere of intellectualism. The great task of our time (we have often described this) is to bring spirituality, real spirit, into the thought-world of people's consciousness. If they wish to live in the modern world, modern people cannot do away with their intellectualism; but they must *spiritualize* this intellectualism, they must bring spiritual substance into their thoughts once more.

Since this is our task, we find ourselves in the opposite position from that of the ancient Egyptian initiates and what they had to do. In pre-Egyptian times the initiates of Asia, because of the natural clairvoyance in ancient peoples, could use the intermediary states still prevalent in people between sleeping and waking, to get the moon-beings that were able to live in people's inhalation, to be their helpers. But during the Egyptian period people gradually lost the old clairvoyance, and the initiates were obliged to create a habitation on earth for their helpers because these moon-beings had gradually become shelterless on earth, as I described yesterday. And I said that the habitations the Egyptian initiates created for these moon-beings were mummified human bodies, were mummies. Mummies therefore really played the greatest role imaginable during the historical development of the third post-Atlantean epoch. In the mummies there lived those elemental spirits without which the initiates could barely do anything on earth in the sphere of societal relations among people. Thus what had been very possible in the conditions of more ancient times—i.e. making helpers out of the moon-beings that lived in people's inhalation, for the spiritual guidance of earthly development—was then effected by way of a substitute, by a surrogate in ancient Egypt, by what was then done by the elemental spirits that had their habitation in mummies.

Today we are in the opposite position. The Egyptian initiate looked back to a former time for whose features he had to find a substitute. We must look to a future where there will once again be people who live with the spiritual world, people who carry the impulses of their morality in their individual character, as I have described in my book *The Philosophy of Freedom.*[14] I discuss in the book how moral impulses are born in the individual human being and must work into the world out of the human individual. They will only be able to do this when the exhalation of these individuals is configured in such a way that images [or reflections] of this morality and moral disposition are imprinted by the exhaled air into external cosmic life. Just as in inhalation cosmic etheric forms enter the human being and work to maintain our organs, as I described yesterday, so must what takes shape in human beings themselves, what is released as the form of their inner organs by leading an intellectualistic life, imprint itself as impulse in exhalation, must enter the external cosmos in our exhaled air.

And one day when this earth has atomized into space, a life must exist that is formed in the cosmic ether because the moral impulses in people—which, as you know, must arise more and more through moral intuitions—will have sent out their images through exhaled air into the ether. A new earth, a Jupiter-planet [15] as described in my book *Occult Science*, will then be built up out of the condensed forms that will be breathed out by people in the future. We must therefore look to a future for humanity in which exhalation plays a paramount role, where human beings impart to their exhalation that by which they are to build a future.

Here we could take further something said in the Gospels. I have often mentioned the words spoken by Christ: 'Heaven and earth will pass away, but my words shall not pass away.'[16] I have indicated that what is meant by this is that a time will come when what surrounds us physically, including the present world of stars, will no longer exist, but that what emerges spiritually from human souls will take its place, and the future embodiment of the earth, the Jupiter-planet, will come about. We might complete these words of Christ by saying: Heaven and earth will pass away, but my words shall not pass away—if human beings become so permeated by Christ that they impart to their exhaled breath the moral impulses stimulated in their human souls by these words of Christ, and which will then build the new world from the forms that have arisen from human beings.

Now roughly since the fourth or fifth Christian century, elemental spiritual beings from other worlds have come into the earthly world. Prior to this these beings were not here. In contrast to the moon-beings who played a big role in ancient India and ancient Persia, and who later took up residence in mummies; and in contrast to the air-demons that played a big role in the Greek era, and to whom Homer listened so deeply—in contrast to these we can call the [new] beings *earth-beings*. We can call these beings who will one day be the greatest helpers of individual human beings with regard to their individual moral impulses, who will be helpers in building a new earth-planet out of the moral impulses of the human being—we can call these beings earth-beings, elemental earth-spirits, because they are intimately connected with earthly life. What they are waiting for from earthly life is to be sufficiently stimulated in order to fulfil their activity in the future embodiment of the earth. As I said, these beings entered earthly evolution in the fourth or fifth Christian century. I have also stressed in public lectures and elsewhere that remnants of the old clairvoyance lasted even after the Mystery of Golgotha. And there were still external human activities, cultic rituals and the like, by which these beings that had been drawn, to put it rather trivially, into earthly development were able to advance. But the tendency of these beings is to help people become strongly individual when they have a moral idea, to configure their whole organism in such a way that this moral idea in the person can become part of their temperament, part of their character, the way their blood is configured, so that they can draw their moral idea, their whole moral quality, from the configuration of their blood.

These elemental earth-beings can become significant helpers precisely for the human being entering more and more into individual freedom. But these beings have a great obstacle, indeed an enormous obstacle. If what we say is to be based on real experience of the spiritual world rather than on theories that can never be taken fully seriously, we really cannot do otherwise than to talk of these spiritual beings in the way we speak about people, because they are really on the earth just as human beings are. So we can indeed say that these beings feel particularly misled by that which is human heredity. And where the superstition about heredity is particularly intense, it goes against all the inner moods and tendencies of these beings, who are very passionate. As mentioned, you have to accept this paradox, for we have to speak about these beings in the way we do about people. When Ibsen,[17] for example, presented his play *Ghosts*, which is positively fixated on the superstitious theory of heredity, these beings simply went wild. If I may express myself somewhat figuratively, I would say: Ibsen's dishevelled hair, his wild beard, his strange gaze, his twisted mouth, all came from the ruffling up that these beings carried out on Ibsen, because they couldn't bear him, because in this respect he was such a modern mind that firmly maintained the superstition of heredity. You know that when we succumb to this ghost theory we think we carry inherited predispositions in our blood from our parents, grandparents and so on, which we cannot get rid of, that we are the type of person we are only through the inherited disposition we carry in ourselves. What Ibsen brought to the fore in a grotesque poetical form, but with a certain grandeur, is something that pervades the whole of modern science. It really suffers under this superstition of heredity. What must become second nature in the modern person is that he gets away from inherited characteristics, that he doesn't remain stuck to the superstitious belief that everything comes from the blood that flows down to him from his ancestors. He needs to start to exercise his own individuality so that his moral impulses adhere to him as an individual human being in this earthly life, and he can become creative and productive through his own individual moral impulses. These beings serve this purpose, and can one day become our helpers.

Things for these beings in the modern world are not like they once were for the moon-beings who were shelterless and therefore had to find housing in mummies. Rather, things for these beings, whom we look upon as the hope for the future of humanity, are such that although they are not shelterless in humanity, they are like lost pilgrims who stray here and there, and everywhere find circumstances that are not conducive to them. Wherever they go they feel repelled, and above all from the heads of academics. They don't want to come anywhere near these heads. On all highways and byways things are uncomfortable for them, for the belief in the omnipotence of matter is most especially abhorrent to them. The belief in the omnipotence of matter is connected with the intellectualistic fall, with the fact that people want to hang on to thoughts that, fundamentally speaking, are nothing, because they are only reflections and people are not aware of the real substance of their content at all.

Just as the Egyptian initiates had to consider how to accommodate the [moon-]beings that had become shelterless, so we are called upon to make it possible for the beings I have just spoken about to find the whole earth hospitable for them and not inhospitable.

The worst thing of all that these beings can encounter is modern machinery [or modern mechanisms]. Modern machines are like a second earth, but an earth devoid of spirit. There is a spiritual element in minerals, plants, and animals; in machines there are only reflected thoughts. Modern machinery is something that causes continuous pain to these beings as they wander the earth, so that nowadays people's exhalation during the night occurs predominantly in a completely chaotic way.

These beings that should actually find their way in the exhaled air, in the carbon dioxide that comes from human beings, find the way barred on all sides by what is carried out by the intellectualism in the world. As much as modern people push against it, as much as they want to avoid it, there is only one thing that can counter this: the endeavour to spiritualize what people themselves do in the external world. But people must first be educated to this. It will be difficult for them. A person who is merely intelligent—modern people are very intelligent—actually knows nothing, because intelligence alone can't help one to knowledge. And such people that surround themselves with machines in which reflected thoughts are living, are actually in danger of losing themselves more and more, of no longer having themselves in their possession, of no longer knowing anything about themselves. They must first be filled once more with a certain substantiality. What these modern intellectualistic people must attain, and by which they must educate themselves, is inner intellectual morality. (I will say what I mean by this shortly.)

People today are terribly clever, but there is actually not much substance in cleverness. One can hear these terribly clever people saying all sorts of things, and they are extraordinarily proud of what they say. We don't have to go far to find examples. For instance, something very curious is currently playing a role in European literature: an exchange of letters, written in Russian, between two people, Gershenzon and Ivanov.[18] The situation in literary form is that they are two people sharing one and the same room. But they are evidently both so exceedingly clever that when they talk to one another their thoughts burst against each other and neither listens to the other because they always both talk at the same time. Otherwise I could not imagine why they should write letters to each other since they are both sitting in the same room, one in one corner and the other in the corner diagonally opposite. So, there they are, writing each other letters. There is nothing in these letters, absolutely nothing. They are very long, a huge number of words is expended, but there is nothing in them. What is said there by one of the writers is roughly: Yes, we have grown far too clever. We have art, we have religion, and we have science, we've acquired all that. We have grown terribly clever.

Yet when one reads this person's writings, who is so terribly proud of his cleverness, one is astonished at how stupid the person is, even though to modern eyes he is clever. In fact, he is so terribly clever in his opinion that he has reached the point where he no longer knows what to do with his cleverness. He longs for the past when people did not yet have religious ideas, nor science, nor art and so on, and thus lived in a completely primitive way.

And the other person can't accept this. It seems to him that all the hotchpotch of culture that continues to develop must show certain fundamental ideas if it is to amount to anything. In short, both men talk about nothing, about absolutely nothing. But they use many words and are tremendously clever.

This is just one example. There are plenty more.

One might say that at last intellectualism has reached the point when it can have discussions like this. It is roughly analogous to someone wanting to sow oats in a field and discussing with someone else whether oats should be sown or not. It doesn't occur to anyone nowadays that they should sow something themselves in culture and civilization, but everyone criticizes what happens, what ought not to have happened, and what should happen differently according to their ideas. So now they start their discussion: Should one grow oats? Wheat had been grown there sometime previously. Should one grow oats in a field where previously wheat had been grown, or has the field been depleted by the previous wheat crop? Isn't the idea of growing oats complicated by the fact that people used to live there who knew that wheat had been grown there? Yet, on the other hand, didn't these people seem to others to be very nice people? Shouldn't one take into account that they were very nice people?

This is roughly how it goes because no one realizes that they should get on and sow the oats. For our culture to be of value, so that no one goes back to Adam or longs for the end of the earth, let no one who has something to plant into this culture sit and write letters to his neighbour as is done in this exchange! It is one of the laziest products of modern intellectual life. It is really symptomatic of the decay in the modern life of thought.

We must look at these things clear-sightedly. People who are engaged in life can often do a great deal; but they must do what is appropriate to their particular situation in life. There are naturally countless possibilities at a quarter to twelve on 23 September 1922 to do one thing or another, but each person must do what the situation requires of them. This fact must also make its way into people's thinking. We must learn that there are certain thoughts we must not allow ourselves, and certain thoughts we may permit ourselves. Just as elsewhere there are things we do and things we must refrain from doing, so we need to be clear that we may not allow ourselves every thought.

Such a view would change a great deal in life. It would be almost impossible for newspapers to be written in the modern style if this were part of general education, because those who are somewhat firmer with themselves would not permit themselves all the thoughts that are written there. But just as it is necessary in the real world for there to be morality in people's actions, so morality must enter also into people's life of thought.

Today one hears everyone saying: This is my standpoint, this is what I think. Well, perhaps it is not at all necessary for them to think this or to adopt this point of view. But people do not yet moralize in their thinking. This is something they still have to learn; then there would not be such a desolate stream of pseudo-thoughts flowing onto paper as in this exchange of letters. This is all connected with the fact that intellectualism has led people away from real spirit, from an understanding of what is really spiritual. There is currently a very good example of this. I will relate this example before I go on with our subject, which I will continue in the lecture tomorrow.

There is a Benedictine monk, Alois Mager[19]. This Benedictine Mager recently published a very good booklet on *Wandel in Gottes Gegenwart* (Walking in the Presence of God). But this booklet only demonstrates that the Benedictine Order, shortly after its founding by Benedict, was once a great institution. For, what flows directly from Benedict's rules for this Order is still working in this booklet by the Benedictine monk. One can have a certain respect for this booklet, and at any rate it is reading-matter which, compared to much of the shoddy stuff that exists nowadays, could be recommended to many. However, we would have to say that although what has been produced by this Benedictine monk is indeed still the best literature coming from that direction, it is nevertheless literature that is completely outdated.

This Mager has now found himself wanting to talk about anthroposophy. All sorts of people talk about anthroposophy at the moment from the most varied standpoints. They can't prohibit themselves from doing this even in their thoughts because they don't realize they have not the slightest understanding of it. But what Mager writes about anthroposophy is actually not among the worst. We need to look at this more closely because it is characteristic of the intellectualism of our time.

Mager says: Anthroposophists wish to develop their human cognitive faculties in such a way that they can really perceive the spiritual. Indeed, this *is* what anthroposophy wishes, and also what it does. But now Mager says: It would be an exceptionally good thing if people could really attain perception of the spiritual world. But they can't—so he says—it's just not possible. He is even of the view that in principle it is not impossible, but that people in general are not able to really reach perception of the spiritual world. And he demonstrates that he is not against this in principle by saying: There have been two individuals who were really able to develop their human cognitive faculties to the point where they could see into the spiritual world. And these two human individuals, in his view, were Buddha [20] and Plotinus.[21]

It is very curious that in the view of a Catholic Benedictine monk, the only two people who could really see into the spiritual world were Buddha and Plotinus—Plotinus whom the Catholic Church naturally regards as a fantasist and a heretic, and Buddha who was among those whom, in the Middle Ages, one had to renounce upon oath.[22] Buddha was among the three greatest beings that had to be renounced. And yet Mager says of these two individuals that they were able to develop their souls to the point of seeing into the spiritual world. He even uses a curious comparison, a curious image, reminiscent of the thought-habits of modern humanity, and namely of the thought-habits of militarism. He compares the spiritual world to a city, and those who wish to approach this spiritual world he compares to soldiers trying to storm this city of God, this spiritual world. And now he says: It is as though an army had armed itself to storm the city, but only a pair of the bravest soldiers had managed to climb the battlements. And with that the offensive collapsed.

During the World War we read telegrams again and again about offensives collapsing. And today we read in the arguments of a Benedictine monk how those who recognize the spirit are soldiers trying to storm the city of spiritual life, but that the attack fails, with the exception of the two bold soldiers, Plotinus and Buddha, who once managed it.

And so you see that this man is not in a position to admit in any way that it might be possible to get to the spiritual world. His intellectualism prevents him from doing so. It is only surprising that he doesn't attribute any Christian individual with the possibility of getting closer to God with real knowledge. But in this respect he is honest. Therefore, of course, he would also have to reject something like my *Philosophy of Freedom* because it wants to assert moral impulses as something that can arise from out of the human individual himself. Such a thing, in his view, is simply not possible, for if human beings were left to themselves, nothing spiritual would come out of them. He therefore says that private and public life must gradually be organized according to the precepts of the Gospels. In other words, without in any way understanding why the Gospels say what they do say, private and public life should simply be organized according to the precepts of the Gospels which the powers of human cognition cannot understand!

It is no wonder that, based on present-day intellectualism, a view arises which leads this man to say: It is my inmost scientific conviction that Steiner's anthroposophy can only be described as a skilful systematizing of hallucinations into a picture of the world, as a materialization of the spiritual.

One can hardly imagine how curiously grotesque what this man writes is, who is actually honest, who is even a fairly significant individual in the present time. To describe him properly I even mentioned that he wrote a good booklet very recently. This assessment of anthroposophy is his most recent concoction. Just take this sentence: 'It is my inmost scientific conviction that Steiner's anthroposophy can only be described as a *skilful systematizing of hallucinations* into a picture of the world. The theory of reincarnation also ends up as a materialization of the spiritual.' Well, I would like to say: 'Padre, let us suppose that you take your ideas about God and the spirit seriously. You must therefore locate the spiritual somewhere when you lift yourself up to the spirit. But you will not allow that a human being can do this with his powers of cognition. I therefore don't understand why you are a padre and wish to dedicate your whole life to the service of the spirit. If you wish to speak about the spiritual at all, then it is the spiritual that has brought forth the material world. So if someone attains to a perception of the spiritual, what is this perception like? Someone who sticks solely to a perception of what is material has this material element before them, and what is spiritual then seems to be mere thoughts. [But] someone who turns to the spirit lives clearly in the intensity, in the reality of the spirit. From there, the things we can see with our eyes are just intimations.'

To our padre this seems to be hallucinations. He therefore calls the whole thing a systematizing of hallucinations. It is understandable that it must appear so to him, because when one speaks about the spirit, one can't at the same time [from that perspective] speak about a material table which one can see with one's eyes and touch with one's hands. In that situation it is the spirit that is only an intimation. Thus it appears to our padre like a hallucination. But let us continue: we must say to him, 'Padre, just consider that you serve the spirit, so you must admit that the creator of what is material lives in the spiritual. And what then is the world according to your view? The materialization of the spiritual.' So if he really recognizes the world, what is it he must recognize? The materialization of the spirit! 'But indeed, Padre, you reproach anthroposophy and reject its worldview as a materialization of the spiritual, whereas you have to believe as a fact of the world that it was formed out of the spirit through a process of materialization. Anthroposophy seeks to penetrate this. You reproach it most of all because anthroposophy takes seriously what you ought to take seriously and do not. That is why you reproach anthroposophy. According to your view, your God, in whom you believe, must at one time have taken seriously a materialization of the spiritual, otherwise the world would never have arisen through this creation. Do you really take the belief of your religion seriously when you reproach anthroposophy with trying to understand how the spiritual can be materialized, how it could gradually become matter?'

Just think what an abyss we are gazing into when we have a fairly clever individual of the present day, one who has learnt very well how to think, who has written a good booklet, and we see how he approaches anthroposophy! Just ponder for a moment what is hidden in an assessment like this, and you will see what sort of blossoms intellectualism has brought forth even from those who devote themselves to serving the spirit, and how we must get beyond this intellectualism—in a different way, of course, from how the Egyptian priests got beyond the spiritual obstacle that had emerged in their age. What the historical powers are that intellectualism itself must turn to will be our subject tomorrow.

Lecture 5

DORNACH, 24 SEPTEMBER 1922

An Egyptian sage once spoke to a Greek sage along these lines: You Greeks[23] are a people that lives only in the present, without history. You speak about what happens immediately around you and do not consider how what is here in the present has taken shape and form from ancient primeval times.

What did this Egyptian sage mean? He wanted to express that the Egyptians considered cosmic questions on a grand scale that stretched out over the evolution of the earth through various forms, and that the Greeks had distinct pictures about this at most only in their myths and legends. But what the Egyptian actually wanted to point out was what resulted from the custom of human mummification, as I tried to explain in the last two lectures. The Egyptians maintained that, in the rhythm of inhalation, they absorbed what could by received through the proximity of certain spiritual beings. They were able to give housing to these beings in the form of mummies. We need to form as meaningful a picture as possible of the significance of mummification in the period that covers the flowering of Egyptian initiation-culture.

A mummy was the form, the shape, of the human being once the soul-spiritual element had been taken away from this form. While a person is alive, what is active in their etheric organism, in their astral organism, in their ego-nature, operates in this form. Through what comes from the blood and the rest of the organism, the form is inwardly lit up by what permeates it as human colour. In a mummy there is only form. This form can exist solely because human beings exist on earth. It could not arise were it not for this earthly existence of the human being. The Egyptian initiate needed this form, without the soul- and spiritual element being directly present, in order to attain something which, without this recourse to the culture of mummification, he could not have had.

We must try to form a picture of those times in which people had a completely different soul-constitution from that of today, a picture that indeed is very unlike our present picture of the world. We must be clear that, up until the Egyptian age, everything that people had by way of ideas and thoughts, what they experienced inwardly in their soul, was given to them directly from the spiritual world. People lived in revelations of the spiritual world even when they turned to their thoughts. In the time of the ancient Indian and ancient Persian cultures, the thoughts people had were exclusively those that were revealed from the spirit. They did not think about the external world, about plants, animals and minerals. Their soul-life was fully occupied with the thoughts coming from the spiritual; these gave them sufficient explanation about the world. They lived with plants, with animals, and also gave them names. But they likewise experienced these names as coming to them as a revelation from the gods. When a person in the ancient Indian or ancient Persian culture gave a flower a name, this meant that for them a divine voice had spoken, and they perceived clearly what the flower should be called. When they gave an animal a name, they were aware of inwardly hearing that this is what they should call the animal. For the people of the ancient Indian and Persian civilizations, all the names they gave came from within.

In the Egyptian civilization this changed. Inner experiences moved increasingly into a twilight. People could no longer discern so clearly what was revealed to them from the spiritual world. Consequently they felt it more and more necessary to live with outer nature, with the animal, plant, and mineral kingdoms. But they were not yet able to do this, for the time had not yet come. The time actually came only after the Mystery of Golgotha. People were not so advanced that they could live with the outer world. Hence the necessity for mummification. For, precisely from what was dwelling in the no-longer-ensouled person, they could gain information about surrounding nature, about plants, animals, minerals. The first pieces of knowledge people obtained about plants, animals, and minerals came to them because those spirit-beings for whom they had created a dwelling place on earth in the mummies, spoke to them out of these mummies. We might say that in the period when the gods began to speak less and less to people from the supersensory worlds, people resorted to the helpers who could live on the earth only because people conserved the human form by mummification.

It was actually quite a complicated process. It would certainly have been possible for the initiates to get direct information through the moon-spiritual beings living in mummies concerning what should happen in *human* life, to get directions for leading, guiding, and educating the people. But it would not have been so readily possible for the initiates—because the capacity did not yet exist in human souls—to get information from the beings inhabiting the mummies concerning *nature*, about the plant, animal, and mineral kingdoms. And yet, even here, the Egyptians showed their greatness. For example, they established a wonderful medical practice precisely through the help of this culture of mummification.

When a clever modern person expounds on these things, they naturally say that, by preserving mummies, the Egyptians came to know the various organs they conserved, and thus laid the foundation for a knowledge of anatomy, not only of medicine. But this is only an apparent view; it is not an accurate view. The truth is that in those times the Egyptians would not have been served by logical deductions of this kind, by research purely through observation. This is not at all how the Egyptians related to the outer world. Their interaction with the external world was far more subtle than that. But something did come about through mummified forms being preserved so carefully: the souls of those who had died were bound for a time to their mummified body.

This is the dubious aspect of Egyptian culture which must always show us that this Egyptian culture was in decline, was a culture in decadence. We cannot speak of it as a blossoming culture within the totality of humanity, for it even encroached on the supersensory destiny of people. In a certain way, it chained human souls after death to their conserved form, to the mummy. And while it was possible to gain information and guidelines concerning people from the spiritual beings inhabiting the mummies, it was not *directly* possible to do so concerning nature, concerning the animal, plant, and mineral kingdoms. *Indirectly*, however, it was possible, by these moon-spiritual beings communicating the secrets of nature to the human souls that remained with their mummified body. And from these human souls that lingered by the mummy, the Egyptian initiates in turn got information about the animal, plant, and mineral kingdoms.

Thus there was a strange mood reigning over Egyptian culture. The Egyptian initiates said to themselves: Even up to our death our human bodies are not suited to receiving information about nature. We cannot create a natural science. Our bodies are not yet suited to this. This will only be possible later, after the Mystery of Golgotha. But we must nevertheless attain this information. The way our bodies are at present, human beings will only be suited to knowing something about nature after death. They live here in nature but cannot yet use their body to form concepts about nature. Only after death do these concepts of nature begin to open up. That is why we keep hold of the dead for a while: so that they give us information about nature. Thus something very dubious entered into the historic development of humanity precisely through Egyptian culture. Chaldean culture [on the other hand] kept away from this and was, we might say, a purer culture.

Everything I have just described (which naturally for our science today is fantastical nonsense—but much that is true is fantastical nonsense for our modern science) was known above all by the members of Hebrew antiquity. Hence the aversion, the repugnance towards Egypt that we find in the Old Testament even though a great deal of Egypt found its way into the Old Testament through Moses. By reading the Old Testament you can get an idea of the mood that prevailed towards all the things I have just described in the nature of Egypt's historical development. Thus in ancient Egypt there was the following mood: because we no longer have inner tools for it, we must create external means whereby to receive the forces that govern and educate people. But we must also anticipate something that is meant to come only in the future: namely, natural science. At the moment we have no other way of doing this than by getting it from the dead whom we bind to their mummified bodies.

Then came the Mystery of Golgotha; then came the fourth, the fifth century after the Mystery of Golgotha. The old soul-constitution with its picture-consciousness of the world faded away completely. The time was heralded when people were to form ideas about nature from external nature itself wherever possible. The human constitution was entirely reorganized inwardly. When people waited for thoughts and ideas to come to them by revelation directly from the spiritual world, they felt more and more that their souls remained empty. On the other hand, however, they looked at external things and creatures, observed them, and from this observation—and later from experiments—they formed their concepts and ideas.

And now the task presented itself once more of finding another way of getting what couldn't be got by using one's own human forces. Ever since the fourth or fifth Christian century, humanity has had to say to itself: A future must come in which, despite the fact that through out intellect we form ideas and thoughts about the things of external nature, a kind of spiritualization of the intellect must come about once more, where thoughts and ideas point directly once more to the divine-spiritual, where the force that lies in ideas can be transferred to our exhalation. But this force is not here yet. For the time being we have to rely on the intellect which is bound to the physical body.

From certain traditional notions that today have all but vanished, which history is no longer aware of but which lived from the fourth or fifth to the twelfth or thirteen centuries and then lived on in a fairly hidden form in human civilization—[from these notions] a kind of mummification was created that is analogous to Egyptian mummies but which, because it is nevertheless different from Egyptian mummies, is not recognized as such.

Modern humanity would have got nothing from conserving the human form in a mummy in the way done by the Egyptians. They had to conserve something else, and what they conserved was ancient rituals, primarily pre-Christian rituals. When, particularly from the fourteenth and fifteenth century onwards, the complete intellectualization of culture came about, ancient rituals were conserved in a whole range of occult Orders. And indeed wonderful ancient ceremonial rituals were preserved in all kinds of Orders. We see how rites, occult ceremonies, live on in the various occult lodges. They are just as much mummies as the human mummies of Egypt. They are mummies to the extent that they are not illumined and warmed through by the Mystery of Golgotha. These cults and ceremonies contain a huge amount, but from what was once in them in very ancient times they have preserved only what is dead, just as mummies preserved only the dead form of the human being. And in many respects this is how things have remained up to the present. There are countless Orders that perform ceremonies, have rites and all sorts of things, but the life is gone from them, they are mummified. Just as the ordinary Egyptian felt only a kind of shudder when he looked at a mummy, so the modern person who comes close to these mummified spiritual practices feels, if not a shudder, then a feeling that something is not quite right. He has a sense that they are something mysterious just as the mummy was felt to be something mysterious.

But just as there were some among the Egyptian initiates who used what was communicated by the spirits inhabiting the mummies to do dubious things in the educating and directing of humanity—and there were certainly such individuals among them—so in the mummified ceremonials of many occult Orders there is also a dubious urge to achieve certain things in the guidance and direction of humanity. What came into people at that time by way of inhalation, came from what they got from mummies. I told you yesterday that the spiritual beings used by the Egyptians had no shelter, that shelter had to be created for them in mummies. And I said that the spiritual beings which now, by way of our exhalation, are meant to carry the inner human form into the etheric world, find no path out in the world but can move on paths within rituals, even when these rituals as performed are mummified and not understood. During Egyptian civilization the moon-spirits were shelterless during the day. The exhalation spirits, the earth-elemental spirits that are meant to be the helpers of humanity today, are shelterless at night, but they slip into what is carried out in these rituals. There they find their way; there they can live. During the day it is still possible for them to live with the breath in an honest way, if I might put it like that, for human beings think during the day and send out their intellectualistic thought-forms with the breath anyway, which is driven by the cerebral fluid through the spinal canal and then expelled. But during the night, when people are not thinking, no thought-forms are sent out; there are no little etheric ships, as it were, on which the earth-spirits can travel out from human beings into the cosmos, in order to imprint their etheric form into the etheric cosmos.

Thus, through such mummified rituals, human beings create the paths and directions for these earth-demons to find. There is good reason for this. What all sorts of occult Orders have acquired in more modern times, namely since the rise of intellectualism, has a reason similar to the emergence of mummification in Egypt. For, the human being cannot cognize what is in external nature without himself, without his own form. When the Egyptians had to create a knowledge of nature, they could have the human form before them in a mummy. When the human being in more modern times had to receive something that was not merely a passively powerless thought elaborated by human intellectualism but something that could go out into the cosmos in order to become active, it became necessary for people to have something symbolic out there, something that symbolizes what actually ought to take shape in them spiritually.

These forms practised as ritual in lodges are now also devoid of soul. Just as there was no human soul living in the mummy, so the soul-element that was once present in these practices when they were carried out by the old initiates, is no longer alive in them. At that time direct spiritual life pulsated through the rituals which flowed from the human being into the ceremony. There man and ceremony were one. Just compare this with how externalized have become the rites and rituals of modern people in the modern Orders.

But here there is something new that approaches the modern person. The modern person cannot get out of his intellect, just as the Egyptian couldn't get into the intellectual element. The ancient

Egyptian needed human bodies, albeit dead ones, in order for them to convey a knowledge of nature to him. The modern person by contrast needs something that can convey a knowledge of the spirit: a spiritual science.

Here I will disregard entirely the occult Orders (and there are many of them) that are completely mummified, that practise out of a cultural coquetry and have no deeper foundations. But even now there exist, and have always existed—particularly up to the first half of the nineteenth century—very serious groups of Orders that conveyed more, for example, than the average Freemason of the present day receives from his Order. And they were indeed able to convey more because in the hierarchy of angeloi in the spiritual world there are certain needs which are of little interest to us on the earth but which are of great importance in our pre-earthly existence. Beings in the hierarchy of angeloi have certain needs with regard to knowledge which they can only satisfy by bringing human souls on a sort of probationary basis, before they actually come down from their pre-earthly existence into earthly existence, precisely to where these serious occult Orders are to be found.

In certain lodges that worked with ancient rituals it was very definitely the case that a person who was really able to follow what was going on could say to themself: The soul of a human being is already present here who will only come down to the earth in the future. Before the human individual comes down to the earth, the soul of this individual visits such an occult lodge, and one can attain an extraordinary amount from it at a feeling level. Just as the human soul buzzed and fluttered around its mummy, so the spirits of human beings who are not yet born buzz and flutter around the occult lodges as though in an existence that precedes [their birth]. This does not show itself in intellectual thoughts—because modern people have these anyway, they have no extra need for these—but when they are in their occult lodges with the right mood of soul, they receive communications from people not yet born, from people who are still in their pre-earthly existence but who can be present now through the ritual. And these people feel the spiritual world, and can speak from the spiritual world.

There is something in the biography of Goethe that makes an extraordinarily significant impression on anyone who has a feeling for such things, particularly when people unwittingly say what is correct, when out of a certain perception they draw attention semi-consciously, as it were, to what is correct. In this connection Karl Julius Schröer,[24] whom you have often heard me speak of, was particularly remarkable when he spoke about Goethe. When he presented to his audience Goethe's biography alongside Goethe's works, he always said something that astonished one, that always grabbed one's attention. He said: Goethe re-experienced things, and was rejuvenated by the experience. Thus Schröer presented Goethe as an individual who, having become young at the age of seven, had another experience at the age of 14 and was taken back a little farther into his childhood by this experience. Goethe rejuvenated himself. And then, let's say, at the age of 21, he rejuvenated himself once again. And this indeed is how Schröer described Goethe, as though stage by stage Goethe had undergone these processes of rejuvenation.

And then look at Goethe's biography: there is some substance to this idea of this rejuvenation process happening within him. Even when Goethe was the stout privy councillor in Weimar with a double chin, even at the time when he made a somewhat curmudgeonly impression on certain people (many things are known that are not particularly nice with regard to Goethe's personal interaction with other people), even then it came over him more and more, and even in ripe old age he underwent a rejuvenation. And in the end he would truly not have been able to write what he wrote in advanced old age in Part Two of *Faust* if he had not undergone such a rejuvenation. For, the Goethe around the year 1816 or 1817 was not a person one could imagine writing what Goethe later wrote in Part Two of *Faust* in 1824. That really was a rejuvenating makeover. Goethe even had an inkling of this years before when he had Faust drink a Draught of Youth. There is something autobiographical here. And when we examine how it was that Goethe came to something like this, we see that it was through his membership of a lodge.[25] The respectable people of Weimar—with the exception at most of Wieland, Chancellor von Müller and a few others—were members of a lodge, as such people usually are. A respectable official in Weimar cannot do otherwise than go to church on Sundays and, as the exact opposite, also be a member of the lodge. That was the done thing at that time, at least in those circles. But this is not how it was for Goethe,[26] nor for Chancellor von Müller[27] or Wieland[28] and a few others; they really went through a rejuvenation process because in their souls they communicated with still-unborn human children.

Just as the Egyptian temple priests had converse with human souls after their death, so these individuals had converse with people before their birth. And these people, before their birth, are able to bring something of a spiritual nature into the world of the present. They don't bring anything intellectualistic; they bring spiritual things which people then absorb through their feeling and which become part of their whole life.

So we can say that the first thing humanity learnt from intellectualism in its historical development was what the Egyptians learnt from the dead. And in turn, the first thing that was learnt about the spiritual in more modern times is what outstanding individuals received from unborn human beings in their initiation-teachings in occult lodges. There is a remarkable correspondence between these two. Just notice when you engage in Goethe's works how sometimes something flashes up before you that seems to penetrate through to spiritual wisdom, which, however, Goethe is not able to express in a thought-form. But he puts it into an image, and the image has a great similarity to one or other lodge symbol. This is the only way he received it. And there are many who have received things in this way. But these unborn human beings can of course only give information about things that can be experienced spiritually in the non-earthly world; they can naturally only give information about the heavenly element, about what is outside earthly development. But because the elemental earth-spirits are held fast by the rituals, information can thereby be obtained through these elemental earth-spirits from unborn human beings. And if there are people with the talent or genius of listening through the elemental earth-spirits to what is communicated to these spirits by unborn human souls, then these individuals who can hear such things, articulate what the unborn human souls say to the earth-spirits.

With this in mind try to follow many of the wonderful things in Goethe's knowledge of nature, or in the nature knowledge of other people at that time in whom such things were particularly alive. Look, for example, at the Dane Steffens,[29] or someone like Troxler,[30] or Schubert[31] who has written so much about dreams but who got his best stimulus for this from nature-spirits. Examine this in the many others who were more numerous in the nineteenth century than they were later, and you get a testimony of what had come among people in this way.

But sometimes something else came about.

Sometimes what the unborn human beings communicated to the nature-spirits on earth was not transferred into people in a way that enabled these people to make spiritual statements about nature and her secrets, but people sometimes just absorbed them into their entire constitution of soul. They absorbed the forces of the nature-spirits into their whole constitution of soul and this then became evident in their style of writing. And where there is a feeling for such things, the modern person can say: When I read a modern historian, like Ranke[32] for example, or Taine,[33] or a contemporary English historian, their style is intellectualistic. Ranke's style is intellectualistic, the sentences are connected intellectualistically, everything is so clever, the subject so cleverly put in its place, the predicate so cleverly in its place, so that the style might even satisfy a schoolmaster. But just compare this kind of style with that of Johannes Müller[34] in his *24 Bücher allgemeiner Geschichte* [24 books of general history]. His style, we might say, is as though an angel were speaking. And in other cultures too of the eighteenth century there is much that is written in a style that does not have the un-individual, the offensively objective quality that a contemporary historical or scientific style has, but has a quality whereby we see that elemental nature-forces are passing through the writing individual, and his style is written out of the cosmos, out of the universe.

Thus something is approaching modern people that for modern times is similar to what emanated from mummies for the Egyptian initiates. These historial occurrences that play out behind the scenes of external history are exceptionally important. We have to be aware of them if we are to understand anything at all about humanity's development. And so we see how preparation is made (which goes unrecognized for the time being because there is actually no longer anyone who listens for such things in the right way)—[we see] how preparation is made for the spirit that is to imbue the intellect once more. If humanity of modern times doesn't want to go completely down the path of Spengler's[35] Western-world decline, the spirit must live in the intellect in the future. Thus we can say: the ancient Egyptians mummified the human form; modern humanity, since the fourth or fifth centuries, has mummified the old rituals in all areas. But it thereby nevertheless made it possible for an extraterrestrial element to live in the ceremonies of the ancient cults. There was not much of the human being living in these rituals, but there is much living in them that stems from non-human beings.

It is the same with the rituals of the Church. For someone who sees things how they actually are in reality, the individual of flesh and blood standing before the altar in church rituals is really superfluous, because the person can see spiritual beings there, quite apart from the celebrant priest, who live in the rituals. Bearing all this in mind, you will say to yourself: If humanity is to make any progress at all in coming closer to what really surrounds us spiritually, it needs to find a completely different language from the one we are presently accustomed to. It is therefore no wonder that such works appear like Fritz Mauthner's[36] *Kritik der Sprach* [A Critique of Language] which is supposed to demonstrate that everything people have thought about spiritual beings is just a matter of words. And if one doesn't want to believe in words, then one can't believe in spirits either! This is the argument of the *Critique of Language* by Fritz Mauthner. For a large portion of modern humanity Fritz Mauthner is actually correct. A large portion of modern humanity has nothing but words when it speaks about supersensory things. For this portion, the *Critique of Language* is justified—unfortunately.

But it is essential for substantial spiritual content to come into our words once more. And this is why for a period in our historical development, at a time when people themselves could not yet grasp this spiritual content, it was necessary for this content to be further developed by non-human beings and by human beings who were not yet born, just as intellectuality was prepared for the Egyptians by non-human beings and by human beings who no longer lived on earth but were already in the life after death. The intellectuality in which we find ourselves was learnt by the Egyptians from the dead. The spirituality in which we do not yet find ourselves must be learnt in the present time via the detour of mummified ritual, which we must acquire once more, which we must at least study. For then it tells us a great deal. We must add the spirituality of the future to our intellectuality by means of these other mummies. Mummified human action has taken the place of mummified people; mummified human deeds have taken the place of the mummified human form. This developed accordingly in a different way, as I have described.

Thus we need to study what is happening behind the scenes of world history, otherwise everything people say about historical events remains for humanity just an un-understood conglomeration of coincidental facts, pure coincidences. But they are not coincidences if one knows what lies behind them. They only become coincidences when people disdain to look at their background. They become waves, as it were, which people believe are just juxtaposed one next to the other, whereas they all rise up together out of the depths of the sea. In truth, historical events are waves thrown up, from immense depths of a spiritual sea of world evolution, to the surface of events that are immediately accessible to human beings. And we should see every historical fact as just such a wave, not believing, however, that one wave puts itself next to the other out of itself, but that each individual wave—that is, each historical fact—emanates from the spiritual depths of historical development that flows from distant time to distant time.

LECTURE 6

DORNACH, 29 SEPTEMBER 1922

I have been speaking over the last few days about the secret of mummification and the secret of ritual. We have seen that there are whole mysteries in these: in mummies, the mysteries of fading antiquity before the Mystery of Golgotha, and in ritual, the mysteries that will only reveal themselves in their full significance in the future, the mysteries of time to come. Today and tomorrow I should like to add certain things to what has already been discussed. To begin with, I should like to present a particular picture to your souls in a more narrative form.

Had you been able to listen in on many scenes in the mystery centres during a particular period of Egyptian development, during the age in which the mummification of corpses was at its full flowering, you would have been able to learn the following. The mystery priest who was teaching there tried to make clear to his pupils how all the secrets of the cosmos are actually concealed in the human head. But they are concealed in a very particular way, so he would say. He would have said: Look at the earth; in the way it is the abode of human beings it is actually a mirror, a reflection of the whole cosmos.

Indeed, everything you find in the cosmos is also found in the earth itself. You only need consider the following. You know that when we look out at the starry world, the moon is our closest neighbour among the heavenly bodies. If we imagine that this is the earth [see drawing], and this the moon orbiting the earth, we can imagine the moon's path moving around the earth, and we can draw what lies between the earth and the path of the moon as this red area [*rot* = red].

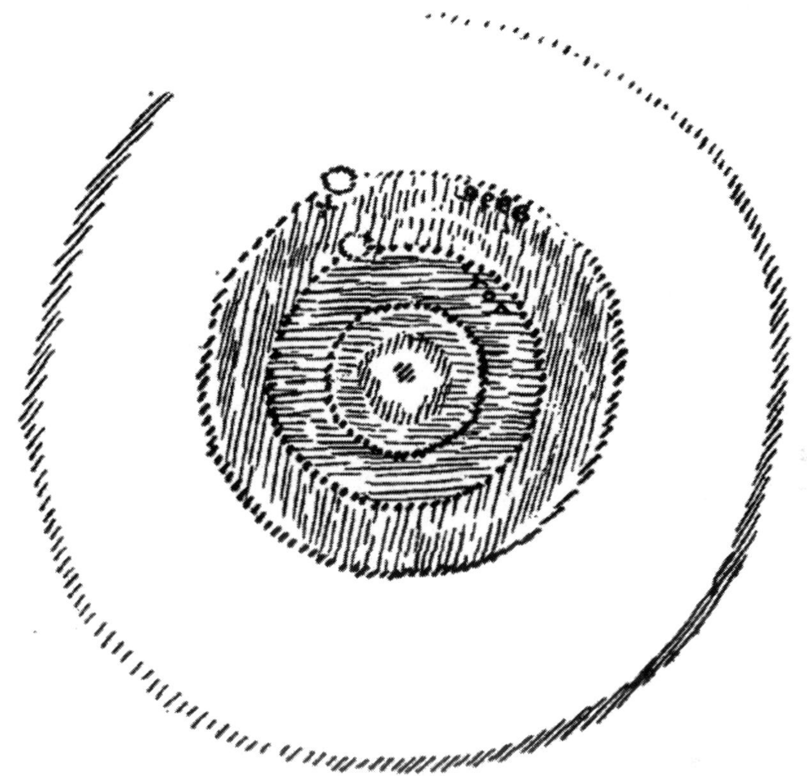

When digging into the earth, a person who knows how to interpret correctly the phenomena that present themselves, must indeed say to themself: What is in the earth's surroundings is reflected, but in condensed form, in an external layer of the earth.

If we now move to the next planet orbiting the sun along with the earth, we can imagine the path of this planet, of Venus (the ratios in the drawing are naturally not exact), and once more we can draw what is enclosed in this area in a more airy, etheric, subtle way [*gelb* = yellow], and if we draw the next layer of the earth, we would have to draw it as a reflection of what is out there [in space] [*gelb* = yellow]. In this way we would get the whole earth as a reflection of the universe; it is just that when we dig into the earth we would always find in compressed and condensed form what is out there in a rarefied etheric state, in etheric volatility. And when we came to the outermost circumference of the universe, this outermost circumference of the universe would be at the centre of the earth completely condensed into a single point.

What I have just presented very sketchily was part of what the Egyptian initiate spoke about to his pupils in the period I now have in mind. But he said to them: 'If we wish to understand how the universe, the cosmos, and its reflection, the earth, interact with one another, we need to look at the human head.' The human head is indeed formed in the mother's body by the working-together of the whole universe and the earth. 'But,' so the initiate said to his pupils, 'no consideration of the head can lead us to understand what is actually there, because the human head in itself does not reveal its secrets.' This human head contains infinite secrets, but it doesn't disclose them to any investigation no matter what form this may take. For, from the first period of embryonic development in the mother's body right up to death, the head is active on earth. But the effects of everything it does are not in the head itself. The secret of the human head is that it does an infinite amount, but everything it does happens not in the head itself but in the rest of the organism.

So, what I have just been saying is what the initiate would have spoken about to his pupils in the terms of expression of those times. He would have made comprehensible to them that when the human eye looks at a colour and this looking at colour brings about a change in the human brain, then what is produced in the eye, and the change in the brain, is an action of the external world. What happens in the brain are the actions of the external world. But the brain does something itself. When the brain receives an external colour impression and experiences a neural process as an effect, the brain does something in its astral body and in its I-being. But this is not apparent in the brain: the effect is in the rest of the organism. And whereas the effect of the external world is a change in the brain, the brain for its part has an effect on the heart, for example, or on some other organ of the body. You can only see what the head does—so the initiate would have said to his pupils—if you know exactly what is going on in the physical body.

The Egyptians knew this, but because they no longer had the means that were available to more ancient times, they had to resort to different methods from those used by the ancient Persian or ancient Indian initiates. The ancient Indian initiates gave their pupils yoga exercises to do; they got them to breathe in a particular way. By turning the process of breathing into a process of perception, the pupils got to know the physical body.

How was this done?

We know how the human organism functions in this respect. When we inhale, the breath-impulse goes via the lungs into the body, and goes through the spinal canal to the brain. In the brain it connects with the other processes that are going on there, then comes back—and it was this return-impulse that the yoga pupil observed. For him it was such that he received the breath-impulse that went first into the lungs, then via the spinal canal to the brain and spread out there. It then came back, went through the various organs into the chest and so on. And this return-impulse was what the yoga pupil chiefly observed. What could he say to himself? By being able through his particular art of breath to observe the breath-impulse as it went back into the organism, he observed in the descending effect of the breath what the brain was doing in his chest, in his abdominal organs, and so on. In the return-impulse through the spinal canal, and in the spreading out of this return-impulse throughout the whole body, the yoga pupil observed what was brought about in his organism by the organ of the head.

Thus the art of breathing, when it still flourished, was such that the breath-process was turned into a process of perception, so that via breath the human being could answer the question, 'What does my head do in my organism?' Now, I explained last time that this kind of clairvoyant skill was lost during a certain period of the Egyptian age, and that the Egyptians had to resort to other means. And so the initiates of this Egyptian age introduced their pupils to the mummy; they also taught them how to mummify the human organism, and thus taught them by this observational method what had earlier been taught in an inward way by following the process of the breath.

But I also told you that even though the pupils of these Egyptian initiates were no longer able to follow inwardly the spiritual processes (and these were the essential point) that revealed themselves in the human organism as the actions of the brain, the spiritual beings associated with the moon-sphere came to the aid of these ancient Egyptian initiates as they spoke to their pupils. And these spiritual beings, which otherwise would have wandered lost over the earth, found their shelter, their house, their abode, in mummies. These were the beings that could still be observed, whose language could even still be understood in this age of Egyptian development, and from whom the first science of nature was learnt. This was done by teaching what the yoga pupil had perceived in an inward way through a cultivated breathing process, and saying: 'Behold your head! It is actually in a continuous process of decline.'

Fundamentally speaking, the human head is continually dying, and every night the human organism must exert itself to counteract this dying process of the head. But what the head carries out in this dying between birth and death is a renewing of the rest of the bodily organs, so that by sending their forces—not their substance, of course, but their *forces*—into the future through the intervening period between death and a new birth, [these forces of the organs] become head, become the head in the next bodily organism on earth. But—so said the initiate to his pupils—you must understand what is contained in these organ-forms. This is why such care was taken to preserve the mummy, so that by means of the mummy's organ-forms the moon-beings in question could relate what the secrets of these organs are, how they are connected with the human head, how they bear the seed-forces in themselves to become head in the next earthly life. The Egyptian initiate taught this to his pupils by means of the mummy.

Thus in a certain era one had to teach in an external way what in the full flowering of yoga philosophy and yoga religion had been taught in an inward way. This was the tremendous transition that took place from the original Indian and Persian cultures to the Egyptian culture: that what had previously been taught inwardly was now taught in an external manner. And thus the Egyptian initiate concluded his lesson with, we might say, a grandiose punchline by saying: 'And now put yourself completely into what you have before you as the sculptural shape of the mummy. In the sculptural shape of the mummy you have only very indistinctly before you what in the human being's life on earth is in continuous decline: namely, the inner aspect of the human head. But you have very distinctly before you what comprises form in the rest of the organism. Looking at a mummy, it is not possible to study life-processes or processes of sensation—you can't study any of this in a mummy. But you *can* study the sculptural form of the heart, the liver, of the kidneys, the stomach, of everything the human body bears in its interior. And now picture to yourselves that when during life you have drawn the breath back in your head and radiated it down into your organism, what is in this breath is the sculptural power to become a mummy.'

The breath-impulse that goes from head to body tries to take on the form of a mummy [see drawing]. And only because the body

weiss = white; *rot* = red;
blue = blue

counteracts this and in turn brings about exhalation, is this mummy changed back again. What one sees taking shape from the head towards the rest of the organism when the breath pushes forward—this quickly-forming mummy-like shape which, however, immediately dissolves again when the breath is exhaled [*weiß* = white]—remains behind, while we are awake, but only in an almost continuously permanent semblance of the etheric body [*rot* = red]. When we look at the etheric body we get the feeling that from the head it is continually trying to take on the shape of a mummy and to dissolve again into a kind of likeness of the human physical body [*blau* = blue]. This is the mobile inner sculpture, the tendency in the human etheric body to take on the mummy form and to change back again so that it becomes similar once more to the human physical body.

This peculiarity of the human being was first taught, as I said, as the grandiose punchline of all the various and manifold teachings given by the Egyptian initiates to their pupils with the aid of the supersensory elemental beings we can call moon-spirits.

So what was the initiate pointing his pupils towards?

He was pointing his pupils to what people of more ancient times experienced inwardly: to the past. This indeed was the strange nature of Egyptian culture that is such a riddle for us today when we think of the sphinxes, the pyramids, the mummies. This is an enigma for us. But it discloses itself to the spiritual-scientific gaze when we know that the sphinxes point back to shapes that were very much in evidence to people on earth during the Atlantean age, and when we consider that the teaching given by the Egyptian initiate to his pupils concerning the mummy contained an echo of what the ancient Indian initiate, for example, could teach quite easily to his yoga pupils, because in those ancient times of the earth every person could be brought with just a slight nudge to perceive what I would like to call the moment of the etheric mummy's arising and its change back into a human physical organism.

It is exceptionally interesting to contemplate the way and manner in which these mysteries were revealed in the Egyptian mystery schools that connected themselves so intimately with human death. This is because human death retains the forms, when these are processed as they were in Egypt, which evade observation during life but which basically must be recognized if one wishes to really penetrate into the nature of the human being.

Now, I have mentioned that in what has been preserved in various forms of ritual since the Mystery of Golgotha we find something similar to what the Egyptians had in mummification. I told you how basically at the time when such things became needed—beginning quietly in the fourth or fifth Christian century and later becoming more and more defined—the mummification of ancient forms of ritual began to emerge. For, when we look at the manner in which rituals are performed in certain occult brotherhoods and other kinds of brotherhood, we find nothing new in these rituals but everywhere the conservation of old forms, of old rituals. We even see how the individuals whose task it is to keep and perform such rituals and ceremonies place the greatest value in the fact that the ceremonies point back to very ancient times, are customs, as it were, preserved from most ancient times. And we also see everywhere that these ceremonies, the effects of these ritual forms, are actually no longer understood. For, what does it mean to understand such ceremonies? What does it mean to understand the actions performed in a rite? If we wish to answer this question, we must understand how the actions connected with ritual in ancient times were understood, for example in the primal Persian and primal Indian ages.

People today perceive a difference when, for example, they touch a rose made of papier-mâché or a real rose. They also perceive the difference when they come close to the rose with their nose. And they denote this difference by saying that the papier-mâché rose is a dead thing whereas the rose which they have picked from a rosebush is a living thing. Anyone looking at the world in the right way in the ancient times going back into the fourth or fifth century before the Christian millennium, would have described what a person did when, for example, they cut wood with a tool or the like, as a dead process. Even if they looked spiritually they did not see the physical matter but something like a dead shadow-image. But in an act performed in a ceremonial ritual they saw how, in what was being carried out, spiritual entities were drawn in from the surrounding elemental world and moved through all the forms performed in the ritual acts. They saw 'spirit-ness' in these acts.

You can inquire anywhere today where some kind of act associated with ritual is carried out in lodges or even in churches, whether people still see in such ritual acts spiritual beings that stream and pulsate through the actions. It just isn't the case. Spiritual life is no more in these rituals than the life of one who had been mummified was still in the Egyptian mummy. These rituals were preserved. Similarly to how the form of the human body was preserved in the Egyptian mummy, human actions, human ceremonies, are preserved in tradition and are also mummified in a certain sense by being performed. Something was preserved in them which can be re-awakened and *will* be awakened once people have found the way to bring into all human activity the power emanating from the Mystery of Golgotha.

This bringing-in of the power of the Mystery of Golgotha is something for which people today have very little understanding. Over the course of time there were still nevertheless always single individuals who had a concept of it, even if this concept was no longer as clear as it had been in ancient times; but there were always isolated individuals who had an idea of how what can live in human beings as spiritual impulse can be introduced into human activity, how human beings can be a mediator between the spirit and what occurs externally through people themselves. One must of course have the right inner impulse for this.

We need only look at a mind like that of Paracelsus.[37] Here we still have a lone individual who at least has an inkling that the spiritual must live among people in such a way that it really flows from people and into their activity. There is a great difference today between what people consider normal and what Paracelsus wanted through his intimations. Today people separate what they do in different areas of life. For example, they practise medicine, but it is practised from a materialistic standpoint. As a doctor, one can also be a religious man or woman in the modern sense. But people separate things. They practise medicine externally according to materialistic precepts, and then look in the separate department of religion for what they need for their soul. In this way religion acquires an exceptionally egotistical quality, for then people turn to religion only when they want to know what will happen to them after death, or how their deeds are connected with what God makes of them.

Paracelsus, in his whole way of thinking, was still completely different from this. Paracelsus wished to be religiously pious as a doctor. The medical act, the therapeutic act, should be a religious act. For him, what he did for a sick person was a combination of an external human deed and a religious service. Fundamentally speaking, healing for him was still a cultic act. And to make it a cultic act was his ideal.

His contemporaries already had very little understanding for this and today it is understood even less. It is always so painful when one goes to Salzburg and hears a traditional tale that Paracelsus was a drunkard, and that one night as he was drunkenly making his way home he fell over a cliff and smashed his skull; that he perished in this way. For the truth to be told, one would naturally point out what his enemies did. For it was not drunkenness that was responsible for smashing his skull:[38] it was done by those who then also came up with the myth about his drunkenness.

Well, the mores are a little gentler these days in this respect—not much different, but gentler. The point is that a time will come in which a deepened attitude will gain ground with regard to everything to do with ritual, with the performance of all cultic acts. And then the appropriate teachers will be able to explain to the appropriate pupils something similar to what the Egyptian initiate was able to explain to his pupils by means of mummies. Just as at that time the Egyptian initiate could explain to his pupils that what they saw in the mummy was experienced in ancient times by means of a breathing process transformed into a sensory process, so the initiate will be able to explain to his pupils, once ritual is understood again in the right way, that cultic acts are something of immensely greater significance for the cosmos or universe than ordinary external acts done by people with the aid of tools (and, indeed, tools also have a role to play in cultic acts).

A time will come when an initiate will be able to explain the following to his pupils by means of cultic acts—albeit acts that have been adjusted and put right, and so not done as they are today.

He will be able to say: 'When you perform a ritual, it is an appeal to the spiritual powers of the universe, an appeal to the powers that are meant to connect with the earth precisely through what people *do*.' An act that is performed according to certain rites is in essence very different from a merely technical action. A merely technical action brings something about. With a machine, something is made. What is made is used in life. Clothes, for example, are made with sewing-machines. The clothes are worn and wear out. In this way something is done that happens through a machine. This is not how things are in a cultic act. I showed last time that, when a cultic act is rightly understood, human beings come into a situation that allows them to interact with other spiritual beings, with beings that are as close to the earth as the beings that spoke to the Egyptians from the mummies were close to the moon. Through machines, through external technology, we interact with the physical nature-forces of the earth; through cultic rituals we interact with the spiritual-elemental forces of the earth. We interact with the forces of the earth that are pointing towards the future.

An initiate will thus be able to say to his pupils: By living into a ritual, by following what is happening there, you follow something about which the materialistic fantasist says, 'There is nothing real here!'—or even, if they are cynical, 'This is just a game!' That may be so, but everything performed in a proper ritual holds the spiritual in itself. The spiritual-elemental beings called into presence when a ritual is performed, need this ritual, for they draw from it their nourishment, their growth-forces.

A time will come when the earth no longer exists. The fact is that everything surrounding our physical senses, everything we see today in the mineral, plant, and animal kingdoms, what exists as air and clouds, even the glittering of the stars—all this will pass away. The earth will then have moved on to become what I have written about in my *Occult Science*. The earth will have to make a transition into a specific future, into its Jupiter-existence. This Jupiter will be a subsequent embodiment of the earth just as our own future life on earth will be a reincarnation of our present earthly life, just that the time periods are much greater. Not a dust particle of the matter that is in the present mineral, plant, animal, in the wind and clouds—not a single particle of dust

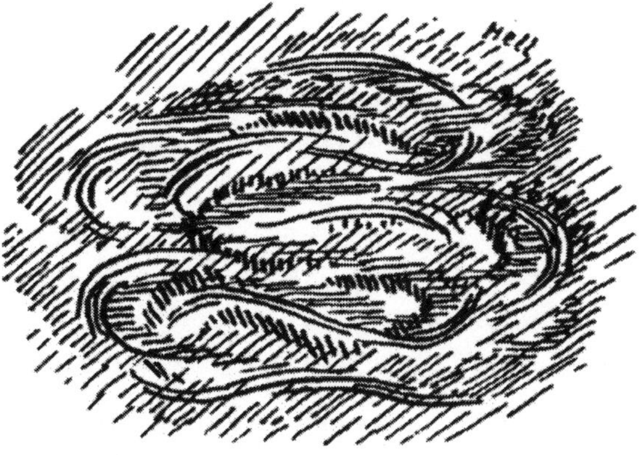

of this earth will still exist, in a certain sense, in the future. All the processes that happen in an external technical way, that occur with technical machines, will have fulfilled their task. It will all be the past.

But in what had existed, in what had been external technological civilization, something else will have been prepared. We can sketch it [see drawing above]. Assume this is our present earth. A great variety of natural processes is going on in it [*grün* = green]; flora and so on, clouds surrounding the earth [*hell* = light]; there are machines doing all sorts of things on the earth [*lila* = purple]; animals moving about, and human physical bodies [*rötlich* = reddish]. All this will be gone. But on this earth ritual acts will be performed in the future that are derived from a proper understanding of the spiritual world. In everything that is in it, ritual acts will be performed.

I'll sketch it here in various ways [see drawing below]. When these cultic acts are performed, they call elemental-spiritual entities into the sphere of the ritual. I'll draw them here in yellow [*gelb* = yellow]. They are invisible to the external eye. But a time will come when all the substances that fill out the minerals, plants, animals, clouds, what is at work in wind and weather, will be gone. Everything that

makes up the earth's covering of plants will be gone, will be turned to dust in the universe, including, of course, the objects with which cultic acts are performed. But the elemental spiritual beings that have been called into the sphere of the ritual will remain. When the earth approaches its completion, these beings will exist in a more fully developed form within the earth, just as in autumn the seeds for next year are hidden in the plant. And just as the dry and withered leaves fall from the plant, so everything that is in the mineral, plant, and animal kingdoms will fall away and scatter into the universe. And the elemental beings, which will then have perfected themselves, will exist like a seed for the future, living on into the Jupiter-existence.

And once again, what such an initiate had to say to his pupils can be summarized in a grandiose punchline, if I can put it like that. He can say: 'Just as the Egyptian initiate, by means of the mummy, was able to explain to his pupils all the secrets of the human head and therefore also the secrets of the earth in its cosmic surroundings, so I can explain to you how the earth in its destruction will rise again out of the beings that experience themselves elementally, and which develop into the future in the cultic act properly understood.'

And there is a grandiose beginning for this view in the development of our time. This beginning can present itself to the soul as follows: human beings have satisfied their hunger and thirst by having before them on the table things that satisfy hunger and thirst. But then the Being came who lived in the body of Jesus of Nazareth, gathered His closest disciples around Him and said: This is the bread, this is the wine.[39] Do not look any more at what your external eyes see in bread and wine, what your palate tastes, what your physical body can digest. What is on earth bears within it the seeds of its downfall. But when you have the right impulse in yourselves you can fill it with what is the spirit of the earth. For then it is not bread, it is not wine: it is what lives and weaves in the human body, what the human being can spiritualize, and what will be carried over into the future when all that lives here on earth is gone.

Christ entered the body of Jesus of Nazareth. Everything in this Jesus of Nazareth was spiritualized. He was able to point to the bread and wine and say: This is not the true form of bread and wine: the true form is the one living in the human being. 'This is my body, this is my blood.' [40] The words attain their proper meaning when they are interpreted through the other words of Christ.

Today and often on previous occasions I had to tell you that everything that exists on earth as the plant kingdom, animal kingdom, as mineral kingdom, what lives in wind and weather, in clouds and so forth, even what lives in starlight—all this will be scattered. Nothing of it will remain; not a particle of dust. It dissipates into the universe. But what the human being prepares spiritually—that will persist.

People today think we bring the air into motion through our organs of speech, that vibrations are caused in the air that then beat on the eardrum (which gets its name from this process since we would not call it the eardrum if it wasn't beaten against). This is then transmitted into something like a movement in the nerves, and then it stops. There was a time in the development of humanity when people still knew how elementary spirits moved on words, when they still knew that when, for example, someone speaks a word in a ritual act, what he expresses in the word moves and flows into the external act, permeates the external act, and that the spirit living in the human being connects with what is the external act and thereby everything happens that I expressed by saying: Elementary spirits that perfect themselves into the future, are present in the sphere of the ritual act.

A person who follows this can also understand what people meant when they spoke of *the word*. Today people just mean 'noise and smoke'.[41] Goethe was therefore justified in a certain sense in having a character speak of 'noise and smoke'. But prior to this, in speaking of the word, people did not mean noise and smoke but that which lives as spirit in the word. [They did not mean] the abstract, conceptual, notional aspect, but the real spiritual element that lives in the word. And indeed there was a great deal of the spiritual living in the word. Christ drew attention to the fact that what was living in the word through the human being contained what led, in the ritual act, to the perfecting of elementary spirits, and was able to say, 'Heaven and earth will pass away, but my words will not pass away'.[42]

And now take the opening of St John's Gospel: In the beginning was the Logos, the Word. Think how the Logos is one with Christ.

What then is bread and wine at the Last Supper? Body and blood of the Logos. And we have seen how the Logos departs from what is passing away, takes hold of what is coming into being, and wishes to prepare the future.

From this way of seeing things, the Mystery of Golgotha can be regarded in just such a grandiose manner as the picture of the etheric body was once regarded as a mummy-form that immediately changed back into a form similar to the physical body. But, as I have stressed in many contexts, if the earth is to reach its goal, humanity will have to regain its connection with the spiritual world. Just as those who preceded the Egyptians inwardly experienced this process of becoming a mummy that immediately dissolved once more, and which was for them a perception of the impulse of the breath that extended into the organism, so in the future there must be a perception of the process of exhalation, the passage of exhaled air into external cosmic space, the communication of what takes shape in the human organism, a perception of the spiritualization of our environment through human beings themselves. The Egyptian said: 'With every breath, the mummy represents a form that the human being wishes to become inwardly.' Future initiates will say: 'Every exhalation represents how the human being wishes to become a whole cosmos, a whole world. By the inhaled air pushing from the head into the organism, the *human being* is understood. By the air pushing out again into the world, in the thrust of the air into the world, the *cosmos* is understood.' We will understand the cosmos again by encompassing the world in Imagination. And we will recognize in Imagination that which human beings themselves put out into the external world in their breath. And it will be nothing less than what they prepare in this way for the future.

Thus what human beings do in history merges with what happens in the cosmos. It is not possible to reach an understanding of the world without being able to bring these things together, for people must once more understand history from a cosmic perspective and the cosmos from a historical perspective.

Lecture 7

DORNACH, 30 SEPTEMBER 1922

We have seen how the fundamental impulses of human history come to expression in phenomena such as the curious inclination of Egyptian civilization to mummify the human form, and, in more recent times, in the conservation of ancient cultic forms which also represents a mummification in a certain respect, but a mummification of cultural practices. When we look back once more with certain ideas to Egyptian civilization and its external manifestation in mummification, we need to connect what we see there with what was said in the course I recently gave over in the Goetheanum building,[43] but which I have given on several occasions here. I am referring to the discussion on the normal activity of thinking in human beings, how they gradually develop this during childhood, attain a certain proficiency in it, and then continue with it between their youth and their death. We have got to know this thought-activity, this intellectual functioning as I have often called it, as a kind of inner soul-corpse.

We have repeatedly brought to mind that thinking as exercised by people in earthly life is only seen in the right light when we regard it as having the same relation to our actual being as a corpse has to the living earthly person who has left it behind after passing through the portal of death. That which makes a human being a human being actually leaves, and what remains in the corpse is something that can only have the form we see because it has been left behind by a living person. No one could be so naive as to believe that the form of the human corpse could arise just by some kind of combination of forces. It has to be the result of something, something must have preceded it, a living person must have preceded it. External nature which we study, certainly has the power to destroy the form of a human corpse, but it does not have the power to create it. The human form is created by the higher members-of-being that human beings possess. But at death, these depart. In the same way as we see that a corpse comes from a living person, so we see that thinking, when we perceive it correctly, cannot through itself be what it is in earthly life, but that it is a corpse of the soul. It is the corpse of what it was before the human being descended from soul-spiritual worlds into earthly existence. The soul was something in its pre-earthly existence which died, as it were, at birth. And the corpse of this soul-element that died is thinking.

And how could it be otherwise since the individuals who best understood how to live with thinking felt this deadness, this state in abstract thinking of having died! I need only remind you of the gripping place at which Nietztsche [44] begins his description of philosophy in the tragic age of the Greeks, where he describes how in the pre-Socratic philosophers like Parmenides [45] or Heraclitus,[46] the Greek world of thought rose to abstract thought concerning our genesis and existence. There, so Nietzsche says, one feels an icy chill come over one. And indeed that *is* how it is. Just compare how the people of the ancient Orient sought to understand external nature in living, inwardly active, albeit more dreamlike soul pictures. In contrast to this active thinking, whose flowering we find in Vedanta philosophy and in the Vedas, in contrast to this active thinking that is everywhere burgeoning and sprouting and weaving through the whole human being in a living way, what emerged later as abstract thought is indeed a dead corpse. Nietzsche sensed this when he felt impelled to describe the pre-Socratic philosophers who were the first in human evolution to ascend to such abstract thoughts.

But consider the oriental sages who preceded the Greek philosophers. You find in them not the slightest doubt that human beings have a soul-existence before they come down to earth. One can't experience thinking as something living and not at the same time believe in the pre-existence of human beings. Someone who experiences living thinking is like one who on earth sees living human beings. A person who no longer experiences thinking as something alive, as the Greek philosophers did even before Socrates,[47] can think like Aristotle [48] that the human is a being born only at birth. So we need to make a distinction between the former oriental, inwardly active and living thinking, whereby one knew that one had entered earthly existence from spiritual worlds, and then the dead thinking, the corpse-thinking that emerged, by which people learnt nothing other than what is accessible to us between birth and death.

Put yourself in the position of such a person in Egypt, let's say in the second millennium before the Mystery of Golgotha. They would have to say to themselves: Over there in the East there were once people who had a thinking that was living. But this Egyptian sage was still in a peculiar situation. He did not yet have the soul-life that we have today. Try to imagine as vividly as you can what the soul-life of such an Egyptian sage was like. The sense of a living thinking was already gone from the soul; people were no longer able to have this, but abstract thinking had not yet emerged. A substitute was created by embalming mummies through which, in the way I described, one came to an idea, a notion, of the human form. One trained oneself towards a comprehension of this human form using the mummy, and by this means people first acquired a thinking that was abstract and dead.

In contrast to this is the fact, as I described yesterday, that in more modern times in certain occult associations rituals, cultic forms, ceremonial acts have been preserved which once existed in a living way in humanity but are now preserved as something dead. You only need recall what you have perhaps read about the rituals of the Masonic Order. You find there that ceremonies have been developed for the first degree, the second degree, and third degree. These ceremonies are learnt, described and even performed in an external way. This was once a process full of life; people once lived in it how the plant lives in its life-principle. Today they have become a dead thing. With the exception of just a few individual priestly natures, even the Mystery of Golgotha has not been able to arouse the inner aliveness associated with the church rituals that have developed since the Mystery of Golgotha. But until now humanity has not been able to bring a fully living quality into the cultic element. For this, something else is needed.

All the present-day thinking of humanity is actually directed towards what is dead. For the time being there is no understanding at all for the living thinking that once existed. The intellectualistic thinking humanity has practised since the middle of the fourteenth century is a corpse. This is why this thinking is so determined to restrict itself to what is dead in nature, to investigating the mineral kingdom. And people would like to study plants, animals, man himself, only according to mineral, physical, and chemical forces, because people only want to deal with this dead thinking, with this thought-corpse that purely intellectualistic human beings drag around with themselves.

I have already mentioned Goethe in this series of lectures. As you know, Goethe was a Freemason.[49] He experienced Masonic ritual, but experienced it in a way that only Goethe could. For him immediate life emanated from the cultic forms that were otherwise simply a matter of preserved tradition. Being able to come into contact with that spiritual entity that entered into [the ritual] in the way I described, from pre-earthly existence into this earthly existence, was a reality for him. For Goethe this was always a kind of rejuvenating power, for Goethe had really often undergone a rejuvenation process in the course of his life. And from this inner life there emerged from Goethe what is fundamentally one of the greatest, one of the most significant phenomena of the modern life of thought, but which even up to today is not appreciated: this is the idea of metamorphosis.[50]

What had Goethe really done by grasping the idea of metamorphosis? What this was, was the lighting up once more of an inwardly living thinking, of a thinking that can enter the cosmos. Goethe had rejected Linnaean[51] botany where one sets one plant next to the other, gets an idea of each individual plant, and then tries to put it all into a nice system. Goethe couldn't go along with this. Goethe did not want to have just these dead concepts; he wanted to have a living thinking. He achieved this firstly by looking at the plant itself. The way he saw it, the plant was such that low down it grew rather crude unformed leaves. A little higher [it grew] formed leaves which however were transformations, metamorphoses of the other leaves. Then [still higher] it formed petals with a different colour, then stamens, and in the middle the pistil. All these were transformations of a basic leaf form. Goethe's way of looking at a leaf was not such that he said: This is one leaf and that is another leaf. Goethe did not look in this way at what was growing on the plant, but he said: The fact that this leaf looks like this and that leaf looks like that is an externality. Seen from within, the leaf itself has an inner power of transformation so that it can just as well look one way [right] as another [left]. It is not two leaves at all; it is *one* leaf represented in two different ways.

And when Goethe looked at the plant [see drawing below], he said: The green leaf is below, the petal is above [*rot* = red]. The intellectualistic philistine says these are two, that they are two leaves. What could be more obvious for an intellectualistic philistine than that these are two leaves, for one is even red and the other green. And if a person has a green coat and a red jacket, these are certainly two things—for philistinism, in modern times at least, is applicable to clothing; there philistinism is at home. But the plant does not partake in philistinism. Goethe said to himself, the red petal is the same thing as the green leaf. It is not two leaves at all; it is actually one leaf in different configurations. In one situation the same force works below at A [see drawing]. Here it works primarily such that the forces are drawn out of the earth. The plant pulls forces from the earth, draws them upwards, and the leaf, obliged to grow under the influence of earth forces, turns green. As the plant continues to grow [*violett* = violet], the sun is there and shines more strongly than farther down. The sun gains the upper hand; the same impulse grows into the sun and becomes red.

Goethe might have said roughly the following: When someone who has nothing to eat sees someone else eating an enormous amount, they turn pale with envy. In another situation, someone gives them a shove and they turn red. Following the same principle that says these are two leaves, one could also say that this is two people—one is pale and the other is red, so it is two people. It is no more two leaves than it is two people. It is *one* leaf: at one time it is one thing, at another place it is another. And for Goethe this was not

rot = red; *violett* = violet; *grün* = green; *hell* = bright

something to wonder at particularly since after all a person can run from one spot to another without its being two people that we see in different places! In short, Goethe realized that the way of looking at things simply in juxtaposition is not truth but an illusion; that it is *one* leaf, green here and red there.

But he looked at different plants in the same way as he looked at the different organs of the plant. Let's look at it like this: here we have a plant of some kind [Steiner draws]. It is in a good position; it can form a proper root out of the germ, a stem, proper leaves on the stem, a proper flower, and stamens around a pistil [see drawing]. Goethe said: The stamens are also the same leaf. He might have said: Yes, an intellectualist would argue that the petals are wide, whereas the stamens are as thin as threads with just a kind of scar at the top. And yet in the broad petal and in the very narrow stamen Goethe still saw only different configurations of one and the same leaf. Figuratively he might have said: Have you never seen a person who is thin as a reed at one time in their life and later expanded to become quite fat? That isn't two people either.

gelb = yellow; *rot* = red; *grün* = green; *violett* = violet

So petal and stamen are one; the fact that they occur in different places is not important and was not the essential point for Goethe. A human being who cannot run so fast, cannot be in two places at once. (An educated banker in Berlin who was having vociferous demands made on him from all sides once said, 'Do you think I'm a bird that I can be in two places at once?') Well, of course a person cannot do this. But the point here is that Goethe sought everywhere for the principle of metamorphosis, for the display of unity in plurality, of unity in diversity. Through this Goethe then called to life the idea of metamorphosis.

When you grasp what I have said, you get an idea of what spirit is. Just think of everything I have just said. The fact that the whole plant is actually one leaf shaped in different ways is certainly not something that can be grasped bodily [i.e. outwardly]. Here you must grasp something mentally that changes in the most varied ways. It is spirit that is living in the plant kingdom. And we can go further: we can take a plant, as we mentioned, that is in a good situation, whose seed is planted properly into the soil, that then at the right time gets the weak spring sunshine, then the sun of high summer, and then in turn forms its seeds in the sun that is growing weaker. But now imagine that the plant is planted in natural conditions that don't give it any time to develop a root, nor a proper stem, nor proper leaves, but everything that otherwise develops in the petals is forced to develop terribly quickly and undefined because it doesn't have time to develop all these things so quickly. In this situation it becomes a fungus, a mushroom.

Here you have two extremes: a plant that has time to differentiate itself in detail, develops root, stem, leaves, flowers, fruits, everything that's possible. But in a plant that is in natural conditions that don't allow it time to form a root, everything is only suggested; stem and leaves can also not develop, and what is in the flowering-principle and fruit-formation has to be done quickly and indistinctly. The plant is almost not in the soil and develops in a terrible rush what other plants develop slowly. Think of a Corn Poppy. First it slowly develops green leaves; then it can slowly and carefully form the red poppy petals, then stamens, then the coquettish pistil at the centre of the poppy flower. In a mushroom this has to be done quickly and over-hastily. There isn't time to differentiate, isn't time to be exposed to the sun that could colour it—in short, it becomes a mushroom. In mushrooms we have a very undefined, quick and over-hastily jotted-down design of a flower. But again we have one thing; two very different plants are actually one and the same.

But in order really to think all this one has to become inwardly a bit different. The intellectualist (Goethe would perhaps have said 'a rigid philistine') looks at a sap-filled red poppy with its plump well-developed pistil at its centre, and then he's required to look at a mushroom. At the same time he's supposed to keep the concept he'd formed of the poppy so mobile in his mind that it can become indistinct, and he is supposed to see in the poppy itself the predisposition for a Chanterelle mushroom or a Royal Agaric. Well, he can't really manage it. In order that his intellect doesn't have to move, so that he doesn't have to make his mind mobile but at most only has to shuffle his head along a bit, he must be shown an actual Chanterelle or Royal Agaric. *Then* he can imagine it side by side [with the poppy]—then he manages it!

And this is the difference between dead thinking and the inwardly alive, living thinking that Goethe developed for metamorphosis. It was an inner discovery of the greatest order that came into the world through Goethe. This is why in the Introduction I wrote to the first volume of *Goethe's Scientific Works*,[52] which I edited at the beginning of the 'eighties of the previous century, I wrote the sentence: Goethe is simultaneously the Copernicus and the Kepler of organic science.

What Copernicus and Kepler did for external inorganic nature by purifying their ideas in order to grasp astronomy and physics in purified concepts, Goethe achieved for organic science through the living idea, the idea of metamorphosis. This is his central discovery.

And if we want, we can find that this idea of metamorphosis extends over all of nature. Once he had got the idea of metamorphosis for plant forms, Goethe naturally immediately began to think that it must be applicable to the animal as well.[53] But things here are harder.[54] Goethe had managed very well in his thought to get one leaf to arise from the other. But how we are to think, let's say, of a vertebra in the spine metamorphosed in its form into a skull bone, thus allowing us to apply the metamorphosis idea also to animal and man, is much harder. And yet Goethe managed it, as I have often related, when he was on the Venice Lido in 1790, and had the good fortune to come across a sheep's skull that had fallen apart in a particularly favourable way.[55] It was a sheep's skull that had fallen apart into its separate bones. And he suddenly realized that, even though very transformed, they did indeed look like the vertebrae of the spine. And he developed the thought that the bones at least can be imagined such that they all actually represent *one* bone-impulse which, however, shows itself in various forms.

But Goethe did not get very far with respect to the whole human being because he did not manage to progress from his idea of metamorphosis to real Imagination. But if we attain to real Imagination, and from there to Inspiration and Intuition, unity presents itself to us far more significantly. And I have been able to indicate how this unity in the human being shows itself when we grasp the metamorphosis-idea properly. We must begin from the same point of view that Goethe had for the flower of dicotyledons—in which, by thinking more and more simply, more and more nebulously, he saw the mushroom—and study the human head as we find it today. And then we can think of the head as a metamorphosis of the rest of the skeleton.[56]

Try to look with an artistic eye at one side of the human jawbone. If you look at it with an artistic eye, in the way it is inserted here [Steiner is presumably pointing here to his own jaw] and then runs downwards [to the chin], you will hardly be able not to compare it with the arm- or leg-bones. If you think of the arm- and leg-bones transformed, then here in the jaw you also have two legs, but stunted. The head is a lazy fellow who never walks, always just sits. And so it sits on its two legs that are in a state of decadence, are stunted. But if we imagine, for example, the human being with legs tied together, then we can almost imitate what we have here [in the jaw]. And if we look at this with an artistic eye, it is indeed possible to think how one might get the legs to a point where they were immobile like the jaw.

But we only see matters how they really are when we regard the human head as the transformation of another human body. I have shown you that the human head we carry in our current earthly life is the transformation of the body we had in our previous earthly life minus the [previous] head. The head of that time is lost to us (some people might even lose their head during life!), but in any case the head-forces are lost after our earthly life. Our [present] head does not contain these. Naturally I am talking about forces, not substance; but the forces you now carry in your head are those you had, if you imagine yourself decapitated, in the rest of your body. And the head you had in your previous earthly life originated in turn from the life you had had prior to that. And the body you have now will really be metamorphosed, transformed, and you will bear it as your head in your next earthly life. That's where it comes from.

Consider a human embryo in the mother's body. The first thing to appear is the head to which everything else, as a new formation, is attached. But the head is derived from the previous earthly life, is transformed body, is form, is carried through the whole of life between death and a new birth, shapes itself into head and attaches the other members and limbs to itself.

And so we can say: When we bear in mind repeated earthly lives, what we see in the human being is his most recent metamorphosis. In what Goethe discovered at the beginning of the 'eighties of the eighteenth century, in the idea of the metamorphosis of the plant, there is to be found what can lead us to a living concept of evolution through the whole animal kingdom to man, and does so such that it also gives us the idea by which we can grasp repeated earthly lives in their form. Through this, Goethe's thinking became inwardly so alive that he partook of the ceremonial element in ritual.[57] There, even though it did not come to full consciousness in him, he had an inkling of how the human being in pre-earthly existence, in a condition purely of soul, bears with him the forces of the bodily skeleton that remain from his previous life, and how this is carried by the human being into this [present] earthly life and is configured into the form of the head in the protective shelter of the mother's body.

Goethe did not realize this but he had had an intimation of it and applied it initially to what was simplest, to plant life. He could do this because his times were not yet sufficiently mature, did not extend as far as they can be extended today, namely to an apprehension of the transformation in the human being from one earthly life to the other. It is usually said with some pity that Goethe developed this theory of metamorphosis because his artistic nature got in the way. Pedants and philistines say this out of pity. But one who is not a pedant or philistine must say with enthusiasm that Goethe was able to combine science with art, and precisely because of this arrived at mobile concepts. But, so the philistine dialectician argues, you can't understand nature like this. According to him one has to have rigidly logical, strictly logical concepts.

But what if nature is an artist? The whole of natural science, which excludes art and only pursues external concepts, could bypass it, as related to me in a conversation I once had with a Munich artist who was a contemporary of the great aesthetician Carrière.[58] He said: 'In our youth, we artists didn't go to Carrière's lectures. If we did happen to go to one, we left saying that he was just an aesthete wallowing in his own enjoyment.' And just as it can happen to an aesthetician that artists call him a wallower in his own enjoyment, so nature, if she herself were to speak about her secrets, might call the merely logical scientific researcher not even a wallower in his own enjoyment but a wallower in his own misery, because it is simply the case that nature creates artistically. And we cannot command nature to be something we can comprehend logically; we must comprehend nature as she is.

So this is how historical development goes. In the ancient Orient there were once living thoughts. I have described how through a transformation, a metamorphosis of the breathing process, these living thoughts were changed into a process of perception. People had to work their way towards these dead thoughts. The Egyptians were not yet able to do this. They trained themselves towards having dead concepts by working on the human being in his dead condition in the mummified body. We are now in the situation where we must awaken thought once more. This can't happen by cultivating old traditional occult forms but by really living into and even developing further what Goethe grasped as his idea of metamorphosis: the living thought or concept. One who masters living thought—that is, can work with the spiritual in their soul—is also in a position to enliven external human action once more out of the spirit. We will then come to a time when, as I have often mentioned to our anthroposophical friends, people will no longer stand with such indifference busying themselves so materialistically at the laboratory bench or the dissection table, but will have a sense that what nature whispers to them as her secrets are the deeds of the spirit that actively flows through all of nature: so that the laboratory table becomes an altar. For as long as reverence and religious sensibility are absent in our science; for as long as we have a religion that is separate from science and merely serves human egoism; for as long as science itself fails to learn to revere what it researches (the way the mystery pupils learnt to revere, as I showed in my book *Christianity as Mystical Fact*)[59]—[for as long as this is the case] we will not attain once more to the ascending forces of humanity.

We must again learn to understand all research as a conversation with the spiritual world. Then we will be able to learn from nature what really advances us in our evolution. And then we will undergo in a reverse sense what humanity once had to undergo through the process of mummification. Just as the Egyptians took human bodies and embalmed them so that now, in a way that almost evokes a shudder in us, whole colonies of mummies can be seen in the museums to which Europeans have hauled them, just as people's thinking was rigidified by means of mummies, so it must be re-awakened in the future. The ancient Egyptians took human corpses, embalmed them, conserved death. We have to feel how, when we have only abstract and intellectualistic thoughts, we carry in us a soul-death. We have to feel that this is a soul-mummy. We need to learn to understand what was still living in Paracelsus[60] when he took a certain substance from the human organism and called it the mummy. In a small remnant of substance from the human being he saw the mummy. He didn't need an embalmed corpse in order to see a mummy since for him a mummy was the sum of the forces that at every moment could bring death to a person if they did not re-enliven themselves during the night.

Dead thinking reigns in us. Thinking is the representative of soul-death. In our thinking we bear in ourselves a soul-mummy. It comprises precisely what we value the most in our present civilization. If we want, we can go into the museums where mummies are displayed one after the other, and if we are equipped with a somewhat more universal gaze, with a Goethean gaze for example, we can see metamorphoses. We can walk through the rooms and then go out onto the street with the feeling that in the present age of intellectualism there is no difference, for the fact that mummies don't walk and that out on the street people are walking along is just a coincidence, is just an externality. The people walking in the street in this intellectual age are mummies, soul-mummies, because they are filled with totally dead intellectual thoughts, with thoughts that cannot live. Just as what was originally alive is frozen in the Egyptian mummy, so our soul-life is frozen and must be brought to life again for the future of humanity. We cannot continue to approach anatomy and physiology in the way we do. The Egyptians were permitted to do this with physical human corpses. But we may no longer mummify the abstract soul-corpse that we bear in ourselves in intellectualistic thinking. As a rule today, what people want is to embalm thinking so that it becomes thoroughly pedantic and will not admit into itself even the smallest spark of enthusiastic life.

When mummies are photographed we also get a rigid picture. In terms of rigidity it is difficult to distinguish between the picture of the mummy and the mummy itself. But if you open an academic book today on whatever subject, it is a photograph of the mummified soul. There you have an image of a soul-mummy, there the soul is embalmed. We might perhaps doubt this somewhat since, apart from their intellect which *is* mummified, people still have other things in them. This is why they run about, because they have all sorts of bodily and other urges. The image of the mummy is not quite so clearly defined there, but it comes out very clearly today in books. We notice the embalming there very strongly. But we have to get away from this embalming; instead of the embalming that the Egyptians applied to mummies, we need a different ingredient: we need an elixir of life. [We need this] not in the way many might imagine, as something to perfect the physical body, but as something that makes thoughts alive, that 'un-mummifies' them.

And once we understand this, we have before our souls a profound and significant historical impulse. Just as, through mummification, humanity froze its mental and spiritual culture when people embalmed mummies, so once more, in the course of the individual's education, upbringing, and development, we must permeate what comes mummified into the world in the human mind with a soul-spiritual elixir of life so that it can advance into the future. There are two forces: the embalming of the Egyptians, and the dis-embalming that modern humanity must still learn.

Modern humanity urgently needs to learn to dis-embalm its rigidified, dead soul-forces. This is a particularly important task, since what otherwise appears are such phenomena as those I discussed here recently. Someone like Spengler notices that things aren't working with these embalmed concepts, that embalmed concepts lead to the death of culture. I showed in an article in *Das Goetheanum* [61] what happened in Spengler's case. He did indeed notice that all concepts are dead, but his own concepts are dead as well. What happened to him was like what happened to the woman in the Old Testament who turned to look behind her. Spengler looked behind him at everything that exists as dead, mummified concepts, and was thus turned into a pillar of salt. This is just as lifeless. It was the same for Spengler as for Lot's wife. He rigidified into a pillar of salt because his concepts are no more alive than the others.

There is an occult saying that wisdom lives in salt—but only when it is dissolved in human mercury and human phosphorus. Spengler did have the wisdom that is solidified in salt but lacked the mercury that can bring this salt into motion and thereby make it universal and cosmic. And he lacked phosphorus even more. For, if one reads Spengler with feeling, particularly with artistic feeling, his concepts cannot kindle anything—I mean kindle anything at a soul level through enthusiasm. They all remain salty and stiff with a sour taste. And afterwards one has to suffuse oneself thoroughly with mercury and phosphorus if one is to digest this block of salt called *The Decline of the Occident.* We must get away from salt, from rigidification. We must apply an Elixir of Life to our soul-mummy, to our system of abstract thoughts. This is what is essential for us to do.

Lecture 8

DORNACH, 1 OCTOBER 1922

In our last session we looked at certain comprehensive impulses in the historical development of humankind. For our look at history these comprehensive impulses must serve our knowledge like shining stars that can shed light on separate events that have happened during the course of humanity's development. Unless we are able to feel and perceive the impulses that lie behind it, we can only get to know each historical age in a very external way. These impulses have effects. The effects operate chiefly and most strongly in the unconscious forces of the human soul. And what plays out externally in people's consciousness is seen in its proper light only when we are able to trace it back to these impulses.

Let's take a well-known historical event, an event—or rather a sequence of events—that was deeply incisive in the Christian West in the middle of the Middle Ages. It was a sequence of events that, externally speaking, was over relatively quickly, after one or one and a half centuries. In its effect, however, for one who is able to understand the deeper currents of world history, it has continued even into the present day. Let's take the events of the Crusades,[62] which began in the eleventh century (the year 1096 is the time usually given), and stretched externally to the year 1270, or so it is accepted. We see that even external history cites how the events of the Crusades had a broad effect in shaping aspects of life.

The Knights Templar[63] are cited, for example, who became significant for outer life during the Crusades. Religious Orders are cited like the Knights of St John,[64] the later Knights of Malta, and others. And what had its beginning in a pervasive mood for crusading within these communal and spiritual fellowships, developed later such that its origin in this crusading mood receives scant mention, but its effects in western Christian life were distinctly evident.

Looking initially at external history, we know that the Crusades came about because those Christian members of the Occident who believed in refreshing their Christian impulse by crusading again and again to Palestine, began to encounter resistance when Jerusalem came into the hands of a very different people, the Turkish people. Pilgrims travelling to Jerusalem found themselves mistreated by these Turkish people, and this situation led to a general complaint in Europe. We see how out of this general complaint, the crusading mood, which had long been present in other ways, now expressed itself in people coming together and demanding that the holy sites of the Orient, Christian sites, be freed from Turkish dominance.

We are told how Peter of Amiens,[65] who had experienced this Turkish dominance himself, made pilgrimages around western Europe, and how, by his heartfelt speeches, won the hearts of many who then wanted to set out for Jerusalem and free it from the affliction of the Turks. But we know that this initially failed, and that the First Crusade subsequently came about through a large number of knights of the Occident coming together under the leadership of Godfrey of Bouillon[66], who then did indeed manage to free Jerusalem from the Turks, albeit only temporarily.

We only need look up these events; they are well known to external history. But it is a matter also of looking inwardly with real understanding at what was at work more or less unconsciously in these souls so that over such a long period large numbers of people continued, in part in an exceptionally devout and courageous manner, to undertake these seven Crusades to the Orient under the leadership of the most eminent princes of the Occident. Above all we must ask ourselves where the enthusiasm for the Crusades came from, which was so prevalent in European life when the Crusades began. Later, once the business, if I might express it thus, was under way, already from the Fourth Crusade onwards, other interests certainly got mixed in with the affair. European princes travelled to the Orient for completely different reasons; for prestige, for example, to consolidate their power and such like. Nevertheless the beginning of the Crusades constitutes an exceptionally significant historical event.

It is exceptionally significant, historically speaking, when we look at the tremendous urge that suddenly gripped a large section of the populace of all classes in Europe to undertake something which, for European humanity, was tied in the holiest way to a matter of the heart. But people felt that this most sacred matter of the heart was connected with liberating Jerusalem from the Turks, with making it possible for European Christians to have a free route once more to the grave-site of their Redeemer. When dry historical facts are related or read about in books, we generally do not feel the tremendous fire that raged through Europe at that time as noble knights undertook the First Crusade, or as Bernard of Clairvaux [67] and others fanned the fire of the trend by the inwardness and fire of their own souls. There is something of tremendous greatness in the initial emergence of these Crusades. And we feel obliged to ask: What sort of impulses are at work here in European hearts, in European souls, impulses that eventually led to the crusading spirit?

We can only understand these impulses properly when we trace how they have developed over the centuries. What I should like to call a crossroads in the historical development of Europe, where a great deal of what later became so important and decisive was already evident—such a crossroads of European development is the reign of Pope Nicholas I[68] around the middle of the ninth century. Nicholas I, who reigned from 858 to 867, was the Roman pope who saw rising before his soul three spiritual streams like great question marks, I should like to say, of civilization.

One of these streams moved as though at a kind of spiritual altitude from Asia to Europe. We can say that this stream carries forward the religious knowledge of the Orient, in a very modified and changed form, over the south of Europe, over the north of Africa to Spain, to France, to the British Isles, and especially to Ireland. We can take its point of origin to be the Arabian area of Asia. It then travels to Greece, Italy, but also through Africa into Spain and to the West, but also radiates in different ways over the rest of Europe.

External history barely mentions this stream. It actually contains a huge amount, but today we will look at only two aspects of it.

One of the things living in this stream is something we could call an esoteric understanding of the Mystery of Golgotha. I have often mentioned how the Mystery of Golgotha was perceived by those who had preserved a remnant of the old initiation knowledge from the times before the Mystery of Golgotha. We can see this even in the Bible itself in the coming of the three Magi or kings from the East.[69] Out of the secrets of the starry worlds these Magi sensed and sought the Christ-event. They thus belonged primarily to those who knew little of the earthly person of Jesus of Nazareth, but for whom the important fact was that a spiritual being, the Christ, had taken up residence in the body of Jesus of Nazareth and was to exert an impulse for the more distant evolution of the Earth. Souls such as these saw the Event of Golgotha in a completely supersensory way, and this supersensory perception could only take place in souls in whom the ancient initiation principles had been preserved. For, with the aid of these initiation principles, things could be understood which cannot be understood in the natural and historical earthly world. Within these initiation principles this purely supersensory event could be understood.

Over the course of time however, it became increasingly difficult to retain these ancient initiation principles. And thus it became less and less possible to find a means of expression when one wanted to say how Christ descended from worlds beyond the earth and accomplished the Mystery of Golgotha in such a way that His activity works on in the earth's historical development. People simply did not have the possibility of shaping their concepts, of configuring their ideas, such that they were enabled to find words in an ideal form to say what happened through Christ with the aid of the Mystery of Golgotha.

Thus, in order to express this mystery, it became increasingly necessary to resort to depictions using imagery. One such pictorial depiction is the story of the Holy Grail,[70] the precious chalice from which it is said, on the one hand, that Christ Jesus and His apostles took their Last Supper, and on the other hand that it is the same chalice in which the blood of the Redeemer was collected by the Roman soldier at the foot of the cross. The chalice is then carried by angels to Montsalvat. You see, supersensory things are alluded to, and people say in stammering words what the ancient initiates would still have been able to express in clearly-contoured concepts, and which one could only express now by resorting to images. So angels carried the chalice over to the Spanish mountain Montsalvat, where it was received by the noble King Titurel.[71] He founded a temple dedicated to the chalice, where the knights of the Holy Grail lived in order to watch over and preserve what is actually the stronghold for the continued working of the impulse that emanated from the Mystery of Golgotha.

Thus we have something that leads to a mystery, a deeply esoteric stream. We see on the one hand how schools are founded over in Asia where the ancient Greek philosopher Aristotle is studied,[72] and which try to understand the event of Golgotha using the Greek concepts of Aristotle. We see how later, in a poetical work such as *Parzival*,[73] an attempt is made out of European civilization to encompass in pictorial words what was living in this stream. We see how everything that lived in this stream illumines and suffuses the teachings that emerged particularly in the schools of Ireland. We see how the best of what the Arabs produced is poured into this stream, but how at the same time an alien element is also introduced by the Arabs which had been particularly coarsened and barbarized in Asia by the Turkish element.

We'll discuss the character this stream assumed through the Arabs, through its ever-advancing progress from East to West, when we have looked at the other stream. But if we wanted to state the fundamental nature of this stream, we should have to characterize it roughly as follows: those who lived in some way in this stream saw all salvation—and we can see this echoed in Wolfram von Eschenbach's *Parzival* [74]—in lifting oneself up from the sensory to the supersensory, in having at least an approximate perception of the supersensory worlds, in letting human beings partake in the supersensory worlds, and letting them know that their soul belongs to a stream that cannot be directly perceived if one's senses are turned towards earthly events. This was its curious characteristic, namely this gazing up into extraterrestrial supersensory regions; this sense that if a human being wishes to be a complete human being, they must belong to worlds that hover, as it were, above the sensory world of nature, and in which events take place that are as hidden from external eyes like the deeds of the Grail knights. The mystery that flowed in this stream was not to be seen with external eyes. This was the one stream which flowed very quietly in the ninth century but which was seen as hostile in the Rome where Nicholas I was pope. The mood in Rome definitely viewed this stream as something inimical, as something that was actually unwholesome for Western people if they got involved with it. There was to be nothing in the religion or thought-life of Europe of an esoteric nature, nor anything derived from esotericism.

Without doubt this was the first and most terrible question mark for Nicholas I. He still sensed the greatness of the spiritual life in this stream that had faded significantly since the third or fourth century—in Italy they had even founded societies for the eradication of all spiritual paths of knowledge—but which nevertheless had shone via various secret paths into the hearts of people and became evident here and there. What often broke through into the experience of human souls from mysterious underground depths of world-historic events, was denounced as heresy. One had the feeling that Roman-Latin culture had developed in such a way that its concepts, which had moved increasingly away from former Greek and Oriental inwardness to Roman-Latin rhetoric—in other words, towards a certain superficiality—were no longer able to absorb what was still faintly alive in the fading esotericism. But on the other hand something extraordinarily powerful was rising up in individual people and in communities which were denounced as sects.

The second question mark Nicolas I faced in the world-historic context was this: that based on all the experience the Catholic Church had gathered hitherto, he had to regard the population of the European West as unsuited to bear the highly spiritual tension that arises in people's souls when they are required to work their way up in the described manner to spiritual-esoteric understanding. We could say that a great doubt settled in the soul of Nicholas I, namely: what would happen if too much of this esoteric-spiritual stream got into European souls?

What was in the Orient became more and more confused itself. Actually it was only this one stream, which stretched all the way to Ireland, that remained the most pure, and for a time in Ireland there were indeed spiritual schools that preserved the sacred secrets of this stream in great purity.

But now Nicholas I told himself that this was not something for the European populace. He basically only wanted the same thing that Boniface [75] had wanted somewhat differently, who had regarded the European populace as unsuited to absorb spiritual life into their souls. And the curious thing was that the actual esoteric content in the Orient began to melt away. The people in the Orient, including the European Orient towards present-day Russia, were unable to connect their souls with this esoteric-spiritual content. But they had a sense of it, at least to the extent that this sense was not thoroughly driven out of them by the advancing Turanian peoples that then emerged as the Turks. The people of the East had a dim, indistinct feeling that everything of a high esoteric nature and which could not be grasped by people's emerging intellect, flowed and streamed into religious worship, but only when at the same time the rites of worship had a real external centre, a geographical centre, as it were.

Thus in eastern Europe, where things of a real esoteric and spiritual nature had been forgotten, there arose an inclination towards religious worship, but with a tremendous leaning towards what people felt to be the focal point of their worship, with a leaning towards the grave of the Redeemer. There at the grave of the Redeemer in Jerusalem was the site where the Redeemer together with His apostles had first celebrated the Last Supper—that Last Supper which then in its further metamorphoses became the death on Golgotha, had been fulfilled by the death on Golgotha, and then lived on in the central service of the Mass and other church ceremonies. And as people became alienated from the real spiritual element, because they did not rise up to an esoteric understanding, in their hearts people turned to religious worship and to what was associated with this worship, to the Redeemer's grave, to the place in Jerusalem. Making the pilgrimage to Jerusalem was seen as the crowning, we might say, of the ceremonial services that could be conducted at other places. All the ceremonies and rituals that could be conducted at various separate places were to find a crowning point for the individual person by taking what they had experienced as a copied image in the ceremonial form, and permeating it with their heart by going on a one-time pilgrimage themselves to the grave of the Redeemer.

Concepts which the ancient Egyptians developed with enormous coercive power, as I discussed when we looked at mummification, could still be understood by certain schools over in Asia, but were lost to the populace. People could not lift themselves to what is the mystery of the human being, nor therefore to the mystery of the divine world as well.

The more the period of Pope Nicholas I progressed, the more one saw in the East an inward, heart-oriented reverence for religious worship and an inward, heart-oriented inclination towards the working-together of worship and everything one could experience and feel through worship [on the one hand], and what one felt [on the other] to be the crowning of these feelings, the greatest act of worship: the pilgrimage to the Holy Grave. When one looked eastward from the Rome of the ninth century, from the Rome of Pope Nicholas I, one saw something that Nicholas I and his advisors considered to be inappropriate for central and western Europeans. They deemed these central and western European populations to have too much of the intellect flooding into human development to be inclined to gaze at mere ceremonies—albeit ones inwardly suffused with heart—or to journey to the Holy Grave. European humanity had too much of emerging intellectualism to be able to be a complete human being in this way. One saw that this was possible in the East, but could not be expected from the humanity of central and western Europe.

On the other side one also saw the first question mark. It was seen as an enormous threat that what was in this stream that contained so much esotericism, so much of what can actually only be fully comprehended with spiritualized ideas, might be brought to Europe. And so, if I may put it like this, when they looked westward from the Rome of Pope Nicholas I, they saw a threat, and when they looked eastward, they [also] saw a threat. In the East they saw a spreading stream—or actually a series of streams—coming deep into Europe, the stream of esoteric worship in contrast to the other esoteric stream. On no account could either this stream or the other be allowed to take hold in central Europe—so said the papal court of Nicholas I. So what was to be done? The spiritual content beheld by the proper adherents of this esoteric stream had to be rendered into dogmatic form. They had to have words, sentences, for it; it had to be uttered. But they had to prevent people from seeing and understanding what they uttered.

And thus arose the notion of faith. The idea came about that one must give people in abstract and dogmatic form a content they can believe in, but without them having the possibility of beholding it. And thus there arose a third stream which took hold of central and western Europe in both its religion and its science, and gave the strongly emerging intellect dogma, but not in a way that this dogma might have been vision rendered into concepts, but dogma such that was merely spoken. People no longer beheld what the dogma represented; they were just supposed to believe it.

Had this esoteric stream, which stretched as far as Ireland and faded away in the new era, been properly pursued, the people involved in it would have had to engage in a union of soul with the spiritual world. For, fundamentally speaking, what was living in this esoteric stream was the great question: How can human beings orient themselves in the etheric world, in the etheric cosmos? For what was beheld, including the Mystery of Golgotha in the way I described earlier, was related to the etheric element of the cosmos. So we could say: Here was the great question concerning the attributes of the etheric cosmos. But for the central stream—the stream that right into the Middle Ages predominantly took the form of Latin culture—what was related to the etheric cosmos was turned into the content of dogma.

In the West there was the unconscious question about the mystery of the etheric cosmos. In the East the great question that arose was: What is the situation with regard to the etheric organization, with the human etheric organism?

In all the feeling and knowledge that flowed in the cultus, ceremony and ritual of the East, there lived the unconscious question: What is our proper relationship to our *etheric body*? In the south-westerly stream there lived the question: What is our proper relationship to the *etheric cosmos*? Previously human beings had obtained truths about the supersensory world quite naturally through a dreamlike clairvoyance; they did not need to become aware of the etheric in the world or in themselves. This is what was so significant in the new era, that the question arose for people concerning the content of the etheric—in the West, the question concerning the etheric cosmos; in the East, the question concerning one's own etheric body.

The question of the etheric cosmos calls human beings to the highest development of their mental-spiritual activity. They must develop the strongest power of ideas in order to penetrate into the mysteries of the cosmos. I indicated yesterday how we first find these when we look in a Goethean way at the metamorphosis of the plant, but then rise to the comprehensive metamorphosis that leads from one earthly life to the next. But in Rome, particularly at the time of Pope Nicholas I, this was seen as dangerous. What was living in this stream had to be filled in and covered over.

But the other stream, the eastern stream, also consisted of an examination of the etheric, but only of the etheric element in one's own organism, with one's own human etheric body. The human physical body lives together with everything that is expressed in the external kingdoms of nature, with animals, plants, minerals. The human physical body lives with all our man-made machines. But if we want to live here on earth with our etheric body, we can only do so in an external way by living in ceremonies, in ritual, when we live in events that are not real in an earthly sensory sense. People in the East wanted to live in such events in order to experience the inner attributes of their own etheric organism.

In ninth-century Rome of Pope Nicholas I, this too was deemed unsuitable for Europe. What was preserved from the West—and then spread even farther west so that this esoteric stream was completely concealed—was only what the intellect could produce in the form of dogma, where supersensory truths could now only be a matter of faith and no longer beheld. But the inner relationship to ritual worship that had developed in eastern Europe was also deemed unsuitable for the people of central and western Europe, and hence there arose the particular form of religious rites that we have in the Roman Catholic Church.

If you compare the form of worship in the Eastern and Russian Orthodox Church with the way worship is conducted in the Roman Catholic Church, you find the following difference: in the Roman Catholic Church it is more a symbol that people look at, [whereas] in the East it is more something that the soul lives into with full ardour. The constant need in the West was to look away from the form of worship—which had become associated with dogmatic thinking—and to turn to dogma itself as a means of elucidating this ritual. In the East the form of worship itself had effect. And what went towards the West finally confined itself to gradually becoming what was preserved in an external way in various occult brotherhoods which still exist today and even play a significant role, but which have been stripped of all the esotericism of ancient times.

How to inaugurate a form of worship that did not penetrate as deeply into people's etheric nature as it did in the East, and how to establish a dogmatic theology that would relieve people of having to direct their vision to the spiritual world—how to establish this double stream was the third great question mark facing Nicholas I. And he worked at it. As a consequence it happened that the Greek-Oriental Church separated completely from the Roman Catholic Church. The real inner reasons for this lie in what I have just related.

Everything I have discussed here was clearly present deep down in souls at the time of the reign of Pope Nicholas I in the middle of the ninth Christian century. There were also definitely remnants of esotericism in the West. There were esoteric schools, particularly in Spain, France, and Ireland. There were individuals who could look into the spiritual worlds and who also had a form of Christianity whose teachings were based on vision. The vision that existed there was later preserved only in hinted-at glimpses of the Holy Grail that kept surfacing in mysterious ways, or of its wordly counterpart, the Round Table of King Arthur.[76] But people had the feeling that it was connected with a vision of supersensible worlds, with an experience of worlds beyond the earth.

In central Europe, and extending into those places in the West where esotericism could still be found, there lived the result of an inner dogmatic theology based on faith, associated with a world of ceremonial that was not completely connected with the human etheric body. And in the East there lived what I have described. When we describe the European soul in the ninth century, we have everywhere to characterize these three moods of soul in diverse variations. Everything else that is spoken about in history is just a fleeting external impression of what is going on in the depths.

But now came the times that followed. The times came when what had become increasingly externalized in Arabism was added, as it were, to this esoteric stream. We might say that what Aristotelianism had become over in the East[77] also flowed into it. And this later influence caused this esoteric stream, which had originated in a very spiritual view, to become materialistic. And we see that already in the eleventh, twelfth century for example, esotericism was fading more and more, melting away, and that this esoteric stream assumed the materialistic form of thinking which, in a later metamorphosis, became the materialism in natural science; for it actually has its roots in Arabism.

The central steam—the actual creation of Pope Nicholas I, which had already been nourished by Boniface, and had found significant support in the Merovingians and the Carolingians, and had been influenced very little down the centuries by the Grail and other holy legends that directed human souls to the supersensory world—[this central stream] came closer and closer in its forms of worship and its theological dogma to a materialistic view. From the purer perceptions, for example, of the Transubstantiation that people had had in earlier times, and of the process of the Mass and so on, there developed that crass materialistic view which was the only thing that could have lead to people starting to argue about the Last Supper. Disputations over the Last Supper were proof that people no longer understood it as it had originally been understood. We can only understand it when it is suffused with a recognition of the spirit.

Thus this western, east-south-western stream became materialistic, the central stream became materialistic, and the eastern stream too, in its essential nature, became increasingly materialistic. The tide of materialism was rising. And yet humanity nevertheless everywhere resisted this tide of materialism in a certain way.

And now we move from the ninth century of Pope Nicholas I to the eleventh century. We must really picture how an individuality such as Pope Nicholas I was faced with these three question marks like three terrible, soul-tormenting powers. For, unlike the situation in later congresses where lines were drawn on a map according to external circumstances, he couldn't say: I order a border to be put here and here. He couldn't do this because souls cannot be limited in this way. He could only give directions, as it were, and give the middle direction a particular emphasis. Nicholas I was a genius at giving the central European stream this particular emphasis. And yet it nevertheless came about, for example, that the mood in the East reached far into the West. It was a mood that ignited the inner ardour of the human etheric organism by means of the sacred rituals of worship, and which at the same time, but now in a more western European way, connected the process of these sacred rituals with the centre in Jerusalem.

The spirit of pilgrimage, of the cross, that reached from the East into central Europe and towards the West, this orientation towards an actual focal point, could be preached a little by a Peter of Amiens and then with a really dazzling passion by a Bernard of Clairvaux. And into the pilgrimage movement in Europe was mixed what remained of the stream from the western aspect via the culture of the Grail and of Arthur, what remained when the esotericism had run out, and the human being was left with the outer form, the human being for whom the earth was not actually the earth but a particular location in the whole cosmos.

A view such as this was indeed prevalent among the knights of western and central Europe, which then associated itself with the spirit of the Crusades. And into this was mixed—initially only like a muted undertone but growing stronger and stronger as the Crusades proceeded—what Nicholas I had founded in religion and knowledge as the actual spirit of European civilization. This is why the Crusades appear as something we can simply no longer fully understand out of the later circumstances. For the central stream then spread. The east European stream remained alongside it and was regarded within Europe as a backward religious stream. The west European stream has metamorphosed into the various branches of occult-esotericism, into all kinds of occult brotherhoods, Masonic Orders and so on. The middle stream was finally also captured by science in scholasticism, in modern natural science.

A person who sees only what happened in the modern era will not be able to comprehend the spirit of the Crusades. The spirit of the Crusades is only comprehensible to someone who can see the impulse that was living from the fourth or fifth to the twelfth or thirteenth Christian centuries, and what Pope Nicholas I had sensed particularly strongly in the question: How do we connect what is living in external events of the world that are directed by human beings themselves, the chief of which is the form of religious worship, with the living stream of spiritual life, the life of spiritual beings? We might say that for European people—beginning in the ninth, tenth, eleventh century—just as the realities of religious ritual had to fall away on the one hand, so the realities of spiritual vision fell away on the other. While the realities of religious ritual disappeared into the indefinite quality of Asia and were covered over by the Turks' conquest of the holy site with which, for Christians, the actions of ritual worship were associated, so with the discovery of America the esoteric mysteries of the western streams fell, figuratively speaking, into the Atlantic Ocean. As a reaction to this a mood arose that asked: How do we fill these things that have to be—the holy rituals and their centre, the site in Jerusalem—how do we fill these with spiritual life?

If you read the speeches of Bernard of Clairvaux, you can still feel today how there speaks out of him a fervent attachment to the ritual of worship, to the external-sensory side in which esotericism is living, and how on the other hand his heart is fired up with what had once lived in the esoteric mood of the West. What sounds into the speeches and sermons of Bernard of Clairvaux—even if he doesn't utter it expressly but lets it be heard in the grandeur of his artistic expression—is what the etheric cosmos wishes to reveal to human beings but can no longer reveal; at the same time it is what wishes to work from the earth in one's own human etheric organism. This is what drove people to Asia, to seek once more for what they had lost towards the West.

The driving impulse nevertheless was esotericism. People wanted to catch sight of what they had lost towards the West by making a connection once more to the Redeemer's grave. The tragedy of the subsequent time lay in the fact that people had not grasped and couldn't hear, for example, what then became the mood in Rosicrucianism—I mean in its true form—that wished to seek Christ in spiritual heights, not at a physical grave. But the time has now come when humanity must comprehend that just as those who came to the grave after the death of the Redeemer were told, 'He whom you seek is no longer here, seek him elsewhere,' [78] so the crusaders too were told: 'He whom you seek is no longer here, seek him elsewhere'. Today the time has come when we must look elsewhere for Him who is no longer there, when we must seek Him by opening up anew to the spiritual worlds.

This is the task facing people of the present, this is what I wanted to add to our considerations of the last few days. And I should not fail to take this opportunity, following on from what I have tried, albeit very sketchily, to draw out of anthroposophical esotericism, to say that in the souls who are members of the Anthroposophical Society and who wish to affirm anthroposophy, there may be a sense of the tremendous significance of the present historical moment, of the significance of seeking the spiritual worlds. And, following on from the incisive things I have looked at here, I should like to say: Within the separate circles of the Anthroposophical Society, may people try to become aware of the seriousness of the present historical moment, and ask themselves in the circumstances whether it would be possible to galvanize the Anthroposophical Society in a certain sense so that it could get away from a certain sleepiness and awaken to real life. Today, where significant things in the fields of science and practical life are supposed to emerge from the Anthroposophical Society, we need this Anthroposophical Society in the broadest sense to be composed of souls that are alert and inwardly alive, who are ignited by insight to the importance of the historical moment.

If at all possible, ask yourselves and others whether it would be possible in the near future to galvanize the old Anthroposophical Society and add life to it from the life of its individual souls. This would be necessary! Become skilful—that is also a possibility! But the souls who wish to ignite their life through insight into the important historic moment must come together on our ground. Do for the anthroposophical movement what many have more or less forgotten to do for it in recent times.

Notes

Textual sources: These lectures were stenographed and transcribed into plain text by the professional stenographer Helene Finckh (1883–1960). For the present (German) edition, numerous passages were compared with the original stenogram and corrected where necessary. The titles of the lectures were added to the third edition by Michel Schweizer. The third edition was newly revised, supplemented with further notes and provided with detailed tables of contents by Michel Schweizer.

1 The lectures of 14 and 15 September 1922 were held within the context of the 'French Course', Rudolf Steiner *Die Philosophie, Kosmologie und Religion in der Anthroposophie* (Philosophy, cosmology and religion in anthroposophy), ten lectures in Dornach from 6 to 15 September 1922, GA 215; see also *Kosmologie, Religion und Philosophie* (Cosmology, religion and philosophy), author's reports on the ten lectures of the 'French Course', GA 25.

2 See note 1. Steiner himself referred to the lectures of 16 and 17 September 1922 in this volume as 'following on from the French Course'.

3 Letter of St Paul to the Galatians, 2:20, 'I live, but not I, it is rather Christ living in me.' Luther translation.

4 GA 13.

5 For more on the inhalation of etheric forms see the lecture given in Dornach on 29 October 1921 in *Anthroposophie und Kosmosophie* (Anthroposophy and cosmosophy), Part 2, GA 208, page 87 of the 1981 edition.

6 See inter alia lecture 5, of the *Französischen Kurs* (The French course), 20 September 1922. See note 1.

7 See *Welt, Erde und Menschen* (Cosmos, earth, and man), 11 lectures from 4 to 16 August 1908 in Stuttgart, GA 105; also *Ägyptische Mythen und*

Mysterien (Egyptian myths and mysteries), 12 lectures in Leipzig from 2 to 14 September 1908, GA 106.

8 In *Die Kunst der Rezitation und Deklamation* (The art of recitation and declamation), GA 281.

9 Homer, probably eighth century BC. See also note 10.

10 Friedrich August Wolf (1759–1824), philologist and founder of the new science of antiquity, maintained the view in his *Prolegomena ad Homerum*, Halle 1795, that the *Iliad* and the *Odyssey* were not composed by Homer alone but by a number of rhapsodists. Goethe's discussions of Wolf's view, who was a friend of Goethe's for many years, are reflected in the following places in Goethe's work (References according to the Sophien edition): *Gedichte: Elegien II, Hermann und Dorothea* (Vol. 1, page 294, lines 27–30); *Epigrammatisch, Homer wider Homer* (Vol. 3, p. 159); *Xenien*, 264. *Der Wolfische Homer* (Vol. 5, p. 243): 'Seven cities squabbled about being his place of birth. Since Wolf has torn him to pieces, let each city have a piece.' Also in *Tag- und Jahreshefte* 1797 (Vol. 35, p. 76, lines 4 and 5), 1805 (Vol.35, p. 194–199) and 1820 (Vol.36, p. 173/174) and in his essays on literature: *Über Kunst und Altertum,* 1823–1832, 'Homer noch einmal' (Vol. 41, p. 235/236).

11 Johann Wolfgang von Goethe, 1749–1832.

12 Friedrich August Wolf: see note 10.

13 Herman Grimm, 1828–1901, culture and art historian, *Homer's Iliad,* two volumes, 1890, 1890–95.

14 *The Philosophy of Freedom*, GA 4.

15 See Rudolf Steiner's lecture 'Das künftige Jupiterdasein und seine Wesenheiten' (The future Jupiter existence and its beings), given in Dornach on 3 January 1915, in *Kunst im Lichte der Mysterienweisheit* (Art in the light of mystery wisdom), GA 275, and the lecture given in Dornach on 3 June 1915 in *Kunst-und Lebensfragen im Lichte der Geisteswissenschaft* (Questions of art and life in light of spiritual science), GA 162.

16 Matthew 24:35. See also previous note.

17 Henrik Ibsen, 1828–1906. *Ghosts*, appeared in 1881.

18 The book *A Correspondence Between Two Corners* by M. O. Gershenzon and V. I. Ivanov appeared in 1921. The writers were living at the time in a shared room in the Sanatorium for Scientific and Literary Workers near Moscow.

19 Alois Mager OSB.: *Der Wandel in Gottes Gegenwart* (Walking in God's presence), Augsburg-Stuttgart 1921; *Theosophie und Christentum* (Theosophy and Christianity), Berlin 1922, page 51/52. See also Rudolf Steiner: 'Alois Magers book *Theosophie und Christentum*—my experience on reading this work' in *Der Goetheanumgedanke inmitten der Kulturkrisis der Gegenwart. Gesammelte Aufsätze 1921–1925* (The idea of the Goetheanum in the midst of the cultural crises of the present. Collected articles 1921–1925), GA 36.

20 Buddha, around 550–470 BC.

21 Plotinus, around 204–270 AD. Greek philosopher, founder and chief representative of Neoplatonism.

22 In a lecture on 31 August 1909 in Munich (GA 113) Rudolf Steiner says: '...that someone who wished to profess themselves a genuine Christian in certain religious communities had to utter the following: "I curse Skythianos, I curse Buddha, I curse Zarathas!"' See more loc. cit. and in the lecture on 31 May 1909 (GA 109/111). For more on the Church's oath of abjuration see Christian Baur, *Das manichäische Religions-system* (The Manichean system of religion) Tübingen 1831, p. 458.

23 See Plato, *Timaeus,* also the section on 'Plato as mystic' in Steiner's *Das Christentum als mystische Tatsache und die Mysterien des Altertums* (Christianity as mystical fact), GA 8.

24 Karl Julius Schröer, 1825–1900, literary historian, linguistic and dialect researcher. As professor at the Technical University in Vienna he was Rudolf Steiner's teacher, fatherly friend and patron. See Rudolf Steiner *Mein Lebensgang* (The course of my life) (GA 28), further *Vom Menschenrätsel* (Riddles of philosophy, GA 20) in the chapter 'Bilder aus dem Gedankenleben Österreichs' (Images of the life of thought in Austria), pp. 88 ff, and the public lecture of 10 February 1916 in Berlin (in *From the Central European Spiritual Life*, GA 65). Schröer attaches particular importance to the processes of rejuvenation in Goethe's life in the lecture 'Goethe und die Frauen' (Goethe and women), printed in the Appendix to *Die deutsche Dichtung des 19 Jahrhunderts*, Leipzig 1875 (see pages 408 and 409), and in the two lectures 'Goethe and Marianne Willemer', Vienna, 4 January 1878, and 'Goethe and Love. Introduction to *Stella*', Vienna, 22 January 1884, both published in *Goethe und die Liebe* (Goethe and love), Heilbronn 1884 (see pages 6, 25 and 30). The rejuvenation processes are

consistently seen as effects of Goethe's encounters with female personalities. In this sense, Schröer also expresses himself in the chapter 'Goethe and Schiller' in *Die deutsche Dichtung des 19 Jahrhunderts* (German poetry of the nineteenth century), p. 8: 'At all stages of development throughout his life we see him undergoing a rejuvenation... What seems to rejuvenate him again and again is his relationship to a certain female personality... The power of love has a rejuvenating effect on him...'

25 In 1789 Goethe joined the Masonic lodge 'Amalia' founded in Weimar in 1764. Its members were almost exclusively members of court circles. In 1781 he was promoted to the degree of Fellow Craft, and in 1782 to the degree of Master Mason. In a letter dated 14 June 1782 to the composer Philipp Christoph Kayser in Zürich he wrote: 'In the Order I am called a Master, which doesn't mean much. A good spirit conducted me extrajudicially through the other halls and chambers. And I know the unbelievable.' In the same year, together with Duke Karl August, who entered the Order in 1781, he was accepted into the inner section of the Order, which went beyond the three degrees of St John, 'apprentice', 'journeyman' and 'master'. From 1782 to 1808, the activity of the Amalia lodge was discontinued due to differences in German Freemasonry. After his son August entered the lodge in 1815, Goethe no longer took part in its events, but through August he remained in active contact with lodge life. See Gotthold Deile, *Goethe als Freimaurer* (Goethe as a Freemason), Berlin 1908.

26 See also Rudolf Steiner: *Innere Entwicklungsimpulse der Menschheit. Goethe und die Krisis des neunzehnten Jahrhunderts* (Inner developmental impulses of humanity. Goethe and the crisis of the nineteenth century), GA 171, particularly the lectures from 2 to 30 October 1916.

27 Friedrich von Müller, 1779–1849, served from 1801 as judicial officer in Saxe-Weimar, and as chancellor in Weimar from 1815. Von Müller was one of Goethe's closest confidants and was appointed by him to be his executor. He was a member of the Masonic lodge 'Amalia'.

28 Christoph Martin Wieland, 1733–1813, poet and translator, in Weimar from 1772 onwards. From 1772 to 1775 he was the tutor of Karl August, then became a councillor. From 1773 to 1796 he was the publisher of the monthly *Der deutsche Mercur.* Wieland had been close friends with Goethe ever since his arrival in Weimar in 1775. In 1809, at the age of

76, he joined the Masonic lodge 'Amalia'. After his death on 20 January 1813, Goethe gave a memorial speech for him at the funeral service in the lodge on 18 February 1813 ('In Brotherly Memory of Wieland', Sophie edition, vol. 36). For the biography of Wieland, see also Rudolf Steiner, 'Christoph Martin Wieland' in *Biographies and biographical sketches*, GA 33.

29 Henrik Steffens, 1773–1845, nature philosopher.

30 Ignaz Paul Vitalis Troxler, 1780–1866, physician, medical theorist and practical pedagogue. 1830 professor in Basel, 1834 professor of philosophy in Bern. See Willi Aeppli: *Paul Vital Troxler, Aufsätze über den Philosophen und Pädagogen* (Paul Vital Troxler, essays on the philosopher and pedagogue), Basel 1929; further Iduna Belke: *Ignaz Paul Vital Troxler, sein Leben und sein Denken* (Ignaz Paul Vital Troxler, his life and his thinking), separate print Beromünster 1948, after the original edition that was destroyed in 1943 during the war (Berlin 1935).

31 Gotthilf Heinrich von Schubert, 1780–1860, nature philosopher.

32 Leopold von Ranke, 1795–1886, historian and philologist.

33 Hippolyte Taine, 1828–1893, French historian.

34 Johannes von Müller, 1752–1809, Swiss historian. See Willy Stokar: *Johannes von Müller, sein Leben und sein Werk* (Johannes von Müller, his life and work), Zürich 1938.

35 Oswald Spengler, 1880–1936, historial and cultural philosopher. He wrote *Der Untergang des Abendlandes* (The decline of the Western world), published in 1918–22.

36 Fritz Mauthner, 1849–1923, writer and philosopher. He wrote *Beiträge zu einer Kritik der Sprache* (Contributions to a critique of language), 1901–02.

37 Theophrastus Bombastus Paracelsus von Hohenheim, 1493–1541. See Steiner's lecture of 16 November 1911 in *Menschengeschichte im Lichte der Geistesforschung* (Human history in the light of spiritual research), GA 61.

38 The traditional legend that Paracelsus fell drunkenly from a cliff to his death stands in contrast to the version that he was thrown from the cliff by his enemies. See Elias Johannes Heßling, *Paracelsus redivivus illustratus etc.*, Zofingen 1662 and Hamburg 1663, 4°, p. 33 (quoted by Aberle, see below). The view that Paracelsus met with a violent death is widely supported due to the findings of the famous natural-scientific researcher and doctor Samuel Thomas von Sömmering. He investigated Paracelsus'

skull in 1812, and concluded that the wounds to the skull were caused by violent blows when he was still alive. In contrast to this, the anatomist Carl Aberle († 1892) states from his findings that the skull was damaged by digging-tools during exhumation of the skeleton. On the basis of this finding and his investigations into the will of Paracelsus, dated three days before Paracelsus' death on 24 September 1541 and published in print in 1574, Aberle maintains that Paracelsus died of natural causes. See Carl Aberle, *Grabdenkmal, Schädel und Abbildungen des Theophrastus Paracelsus* (Grave Monument, Skull and Pictures of Theophrastus Paracelsus), Salzburg 1891. Arguing against the view of a violent death is also the fact that Michael Toxites says nothing about it. Toxites was one of the earliest Paracelsus researchers, the editor of Paracelsus' writings, and defender of his views. He was also acquainted with individuals who lived in Salzburg during Paracelsus' lifetime. See Julius Hartmann, *Theophrast von Hohenheim*, Stuttgart and Berlin 1904, p. 154.

39 See note 40.

40 Matthew 26:26–28; Mark 14:22–24; Luke 22:19–20.

41 '*Schall und Rauch*'—Steiner is referring to a line in Goethe's *Faust I* in the scene 'Marthen's Garden'.

42 Matthew 24:35.

43 See note 1.

44 Friedrich Nietzsche (1844–1900). In *Die Philosophie im tragischen Zeitalter der Griechen* (Philosophy in the tragic age of the Greeks), 1873, Volume X, 'Parmenides', § 11. p.54.

45 Parmenides, (c. 540 to c. 480 BC), a pre-Socratic philosopher from Elea in Magna Graecia.

46 Heraclitus, (c. 535 to c. 475 BC), pre-Socratic Greek philosopher from the city of Ephesus.

47 Socrates (470–399 BC).

48 Aristotle (384–322 BC). For his view on human existence before birth see Franz Brentano, *Die Psychologie des Aristoteles* (The psychology of Aristotle), Mainz 1867, and *Aristoteles' Lehre vom Ursprung des menschlichen Geistes* (Aristotle's theory on the origin of the human mind), Leipzig 1911. See also Rudolf Steiner's lecture on 12 December 1911 in Berlin, in *Anthroposophie, Psychosophie, Pneumatosophie* (Anthroposophy, psychosophy, pneumatosophy), GA 115.

49 See note 25.

50 See *Goethes Naturwissenschaftliche Schriften* (Goethe's scientific works), with textual introductions, notes, and clarifications, edited by Rudolf Steiner in Kürschner's *Deutsche National-Literatur* (German national literature), vol. 1 (1883), 5 Volumes, reprint Dornach 1975, GA 1. See also Rudolf Steiner, *Goethes Weltanschauung* (Goethe's worldview), chapter on 'Die Metamorphosenlehre' (The theory of metamorphosis), GA 6).

51 Carl Linnaeus (1707–1778), Swedish scientist, biologist, and physician. He developed a classification system for the plant kingdom.

52 For *Goethe's Scientific Works* see note 50, page LXXIII: *Goethe ist der Kopernikus und Kepler der organischen Welt* (Goethe is the Copernicus and the Kepler of the organic world).

53 For more on the skull bones as a metamorphosis of the vertebrae see page 316 and 321 of the above work (note 52).

54 See Rudolf Steiner, *Goethes Weltanschauung* (Goethe's worldview), GA 6, 1963 edition, p. 131–138, and the lecture of 26 January 1923 in *Lebendiges Naturerkennen, intellektueller Sündenfall und spirituelle Sündenerhebung*, (Living perception of nature, intellectual fall, and spiritual redemption) GA 220, 1982 edition, p. 161.

55 Goethe's journals and diaries from 1790 (edition Sopienausgabe, vol. 35. Part 1, p.15). See also GA 1a, p. 316, and GA 6, p. 133 (compare with note 50).

56 See also Rudolf Steiner's detailed discussion in a public lecture on 15 April 1916 in Berlin (GA 65) and in the lectures to members on 31 July and on 5, 6, 7, and 28 August 1916 (GA 170).

57 See note 25.

58 Moriz Carrière (1817–1895) was a professor in Munich from 1853.

59 Rudolf Steiner, *Christianity as Mystical Fact* (1902), GA 8.

60 Paracelsus, *Traktat der Philosophie* (Treatise on philosophy) III, vol. 9, *Von der Mumie* (Concerning mummies). See also note 37.

61 *Das Goetheanum*, vol. 2,1922, nos. 2–5. In Rudolf Steiner: *Der Goetheanumgedanke inmitten der Kulturkrisis der Gegenwart. Gesammelte Aufsätze 1921–1925* (The Goetheanum idea in the midst of the present cultural crisis: collected essays 1921–1925), GA 36.

62 The First Crusade, 1096–1099, was led by Godfrey of Bouillon (born around 1060), duke of lower Lorraine. 1099 conquest of Jerusalem and

crowning of Godfrey as the first King of Jerusalem. 1100 Godfrey's death in Jerusalem. Seventh and last Crusade 1270 led by King Louis IX of France against Tunis.

63 The Knights Templar were a spiritual Order of knights, founded in 1119 in Jerusalem to protect pilgrims. See also Rudolf Steiner's lecture of 25 September and 2 October 1916 in Dornach in *Goethe und die Krisis des neunzehnten Jahrhunderts* (Goethe and the crisis of the nineteenth century), GA 171.

64 The Knights of St John were founded around 1100 in Jerusalem, moved to Cyprus in 1291, to Rhodes in 1309, and to Malta in 1530, hence the name 'Knights of Malta' (Catholic branch).

65 Peter of Amiens, also called Peter the Hermit (c.1050–1115) was an itinerant preacher of repentance. In 1095 he gathered a large crowd of peasants and burghers in Central and Northern France to crusade to Jerusalem. In Hungary and Asia Minor however, they were mostly destroyed.

66 Godfrey of Bouillon: see note 62.

67 Bernard of Clairvaux (1090–1153), called for the Second Crusade in 1147.

68 Pope Nicholas I was a Roman of noble birth who held the papacy from 858 until his death in 867. Of exceptional intelligence and indomitable will, he was a resolute proponent of papal primacy above wordly princes and powerful church dignitaries.

69 See Matthew 2:1–12. For the significance of the three Magi in esoteric Christianity see also Rudolf Steiner's lecture in Leipzig on 29 December 1913 in *Christus und die geistige Welt. Von der Suche nach dem heiligen Gral* (Christ and the spiritual world: the quest for the Holy Grail), GA 149.

70 See note 73. The story of the origin of the Grail comes from Robert de Boron.

71 The first Grail King. See also note 70 and note 76.

72 It has not been possible to conclusively verify the events referred to here by Steiner. Some indications, on the one hand, from other statements by Steiner that elucidate the significance of the events alluded to, and the historical context in which this fact is to be sought, can be found in *Beiträge zur Rudolf Steiner Gesamtausgabe* (Contributions to the Complete Works of Rudolf Steiner), No. 99, Dornach, Easter 1988.

73 The most important medieval poetical works on Parzival and the Grail are the old French *Perceval* (around 1180) by Crestien de Troyes (before 1150–before 1190), the *Roman de l'Estoire dou Graal* by Robert de Boron (end of the 12th century), *Parzival* by Wolfram von Eschenbach (see note 74), and *Der jüngere Titurel* (The Younger Titurel) (around 1280), attributed to Albrecht von Scharfenberg.

74 Wolfram von Eschenbach (c. 1160–1220), was the most significant writer of Middle High German epic. His chief work, the epic Grail story *Parzival* was written around 1200–1210.

75 Boniface (c. 680–754), was a Scottish Benedictine monk, then archbishop, Primate of the Franconian Church. He was killed by heathen Frisians in 754.

76 For the connection between the Grail and Arthurian streams see Rudolf Steiner's lectures on 21 and 27 August 1924 in Torquay and London in *Karmic Relationships,* Vol. 6, GA 240.

77 See note 72.

78 See Matthew 28:5–6; Mark 16:6; Luke 24:5–6.

Rudolf Steiner's Collected Works

The German Edition of Rudolf Steiner's Collected Works (the *Gesamtausgabe* [GA], published by Rudolf Steiner Verlag, Dornach, Switzerland) will be completed in the year 2025. The works are organized either by type of work (written, spoken, artistic creations), chronology, audience (public or other), or subject (education, art, etc.). For ease of comparison, the Collected Works in English (CW), listed below, follows the German organization and numbering.

The volumes that have so far been published in the English Collected Works edition appear *in italics with their published titles*; all other volumes, including those that have appeared in editions other than the CW, are set in Roman type with *literal translations* of the German titles. Published English titles are not necessarily the same as the German.

This list is current as of the date of this volume's publication.

A. Written Works

I. Writings 1884–1925

CW 1	Introductions and Selected Commentary on Goethe's Natural-scientific Writings
CW 1a–e	Goethe's Natural-scientific Writings
CW 1f	Editorial Afterwords to Goethe's Natural-scientific Writings in the Weimar Edition (1891–1896)
CW 2	*Goethe's Theory of Knowledge: An Outline of the Epistemology of His Worldview*
CW 3	Truth and Science
CW 4	The Philosophy of Freedom
CW 4a	Documents to 'The Philosophy of Freedom'
CW 5	Friedrich Nietzsche, A Fighter against His Own Time
CW 6	Goethe's Worldview
CW 7	Mysticism at the Dawn of Modern Spiritual Life and Its Relationship with Modern Worldviews
CW 8	*Christianity as Mystical Fact and the Mysteries of Antiquity*

CW 9 Theosophy: An Introduction into Supersensible World Knowledge and Human Purpose
CW 10 How Does One Attain Knowledge of Higher Worlds?
CW 11 From the Akasha-Chronicle
CW 12 Levels of Higher Knowledge
CW 13 Occult Science in Outline
CW 14 *Four Modern Mystery Dramas*
CW 15 The Spiritual Guidance of the Individual and Humanity
CW 16/17 *A Way of Self-Knowledge & The Threshold of the Spiritual World*
CW 18 The Riddles of Philosophy in Their History, Presented as an Outline
CW 18a Views of the World and of Life in the Nineteenth Century
CW 19 Thoughts during the Time of War (1915) and Further Texts on the Events of the World War (1917–1921)
CW 20 The Riddles of the Human Being: Articulated and Unarticulated in the Thinking, Views and Opinions of a Series of German and Austrian Personalities
CW 21 The Riddles of the Soul
CW 22 Goethe's Spiritual Nature and Its Revelation in 'Faust' and through the 'Fairy Tale of the Snake and the Lily'
CW 23 The Central Points of the Social Question in the Necessities of Life in the Present and the Future
CW 24 Essays Concerning the Threefold Division of the Social Organism and the Period 1915–1921
CW 25 Three Steps of Anthroposophy. Philosophy – Cosmology – Religion
CW 26 Anthroposophical Leading Thoughts
CW 27 Fundamentals for Expansion of the Art of Healing according to Spiritual-Scientific Insights
CW 28 *Autobiography: Chapters in the Course of My Life: 1861–1907*

II. Collected Essays

CW 29 Collected Essays on Dramaturgy, 1889–1900
CW 30 Methodical Foundations of Anthroposophy: Collected Essays on Philosophy, Natural Science, Aesthetics and Psychology, 1884–1901
CW 31 Collected Essays on Culture and Current Events, 1887–1901
CW 32 Collected Essays on Literature, 1884–1902
CW 33 Biographies and Biographical Sketches, 1894–1905
CW 34 Lucifer-Gnosis: Foundational Essays on Anthroposophy and Reports from the Periodicals 'Luzifer' and 'Lucifer-Gnosis,' 1903–1908
CW 35 Philosophy and Anthroposophy: Collected Essays, 1904–1923
CW 36 The Goetheanum-Idea in the Middle of the Cultural Crisis of the Present: Collected Essays from the Periodical 'Das Goetheanum,' 1921–1925

CW 37 Writings on the History of the Anthroposophical Movement and Society 1902–1925

III. Publications from the Literary Estate

CW 38/1 Complete Letters, Vol. 1: Weimar Period 1879–1890
CW 38/2 Complete Letters, Vol. 2: Weimar Period 1890–1897
CW 38/3 Complete Letters, Vol. 3: Early Berlin Period 1897–1905 [forthcoming]
CW 38/4 Complete Letters, Vol. 4: Activity within the Theosophical Society 1905–1912 [forthcoming]
CW 38/5 Complete Letters, Vol. 5: From the Founding of the Anthroposophical Society to the Opening of the Goetheanum 1913–1920 [forthcoming]
CW 38/6 Compelte Letters, Vol. 6: The Last Years 1920–1925 [forthcoming]
CW 40 Truth-Wrought Words
CW 40a Sayings, Poems and Mantras; Supplementary Volume
CW 41a Translations and Free Renderings from the Old and New Testaments
CW 41b Translations and Free Renderings of Various Works
CW 42 Stage Adaptations I: Dramas by Edouard Schuré
CW 43 Stage Adaptations II: The Oberufer Christmas Plays
CW 44 Sketches, Fragments and Paralipomena on the Four Mystery Dramas
CW 45 Anthroposophy: A Fragment from the Year 1910
CW 46 Posthumous Essays and Fragments 1879–1924
CW 47/48 Notebooks and Notepads (digital edition)
CW 49 Notes for and about Helmuth and Eliza von Moltke and Relatives, 1904–1924 [forthcoming]
CW 50 [Blank number]

B. Lectures

I. Public Lectures

CW 51 *On Philosophy, History, and Literature: Lectures at the Worker Education School and the Independent College, Berlin, 1901–1905*
CW 52 Spiritual Teachings Concerning the Soul and Observation of the World
CW 53 The Origin and Goal of the Human Being
CW 54 The Riddles of the World and Anthroposophy
CW 55 Knowledge of the Supersensible in Our Times and Its Meaning for Life Today
CW 56 Knowledge of the Soul and of the Spirit
CW 57 Where and How Does One Find the Spirit?
CW 58 The Metamorphoses of the Soul Life. Paths of Soul Experiences: Part One
CW 59 The Metamorphoses of the Soul Life. Paths of Soul Experiences:

Part Two

CW 60 The Answers of Spiritual Science to the Biggest Questions of Existence
CW 61 Human History in the Light of Spiritual Research
CW 62 *Results of Spiritual Research*
CW 63 Spiritual Science as a Treasure for Life
CW 64 Out of Destiny-Burdened Times
CW 65 Out of Central European Spiritual Life
CW 66 Spirit and Matter, Life and Death
CW 67 The Eternal in the Human Soul. Immortality and Freedom
CW 68a On the Being of Christianity
CW 68b The Cycle of the Human Being within the Sense-, Soul-, and Spirit-World
CW 68c Goethe and the Present
CW 68d The Being of Man in the Light of Spiritual Science
CW 69a Truths and Errors of Spiritual Research. Spiritual Science and the Future of Mankind
CW 69b Knowledge and Immortality
CW 69c New Christ-Experience
CW 69d Death and Immortality in the Light of Spiritual Science
CW 69e Spiritual Science and the Spiritual Goals of Our Time
CW 70a Human Soul, Destiny and Death
CW 70b Paths to the Knowledge of the Eternal Powers of the Human Soul
CW 71a Soul Immortality [forthcoming]
CW 71b The Human Being as a Soul and Spirit Being
CW 72 Freedom – Immortality – Social Life
CW 73 The Supplementing of the Modern Sciences through Anthroposophy
CW 73a Specialized Fields of Knowledge and Anthroposophy
CW 74 The Philosophy of Thomas Aquinas
CW 75 *Anthroposophy and the Natural Sciences: Foundations and Methods*
CW 76 The Fructifying Effect of Anthroposophy on Specialized Fields
CW 77a The Task of Anthroposophy in Relation to Science and Life: The Darmstadt College Course
CW 77b Art and Anthroposophy. The Goetheanum-Impulse
CW 78 Anthroposophy, Its Roots of Knowledge and Fruits for Life
CW 79 The Reality of the Higher Worlds
CW 80a The Being of Anthroposophy
CW 80b The Inner Realm of Nature and the Being of the Human Soul
CW 80c Anthroposophical Spiritual Science and the Great Civilizational Questions of the Present
CW 81 *Reimagining Academic Studies: Science, Philosophy, Education, Social Science, Theology, Theory of Language*
CW 82 *Becoming Fully Human: The Significance of Anthroposophy in Contemporary Spiritual Life*
CW 83 *The Tension between East and West*

CW 84 *The Aims of Anthroposophy and the Purpose of the Goetheanum*
CW 85 Supplementary Volume: Individual Public Lectures I [forthcoming]
CW 86 Supplementary Volume: Individual Public Lectures II [forthcoming]

II. Lectures to the Members of the Anthroposophical Society

CW 87 Ancient Mysteries and Christianity
CW 88 *Concerning the Astral World and Devachan*
CW 89 Consciousness–Life–Form. Fundamental Principles of a Spiritual-Scientific Cosmology
CW 90a Self-knowledge and Knowledge of the Divine, Vol. I. Theosophy, Christology, and Mythology
CW 90b Self-knowledge and Knowledge of the Divine, Vol. II. Theosophy, Christology, and Mythology
CW 90c Theosophy and Occultism
CW 91 Cosmology and Human Evolution. Introduction to Theosophy – Theory of Colours
CW 92 *The Occult Truths of Myths and Legends: Greek and Germanic Mythology: Richard Wagner in the Light of Spiritual Science*
CW 93 The Temple Legend and the Golden Legend as a Symbolic Expression of Past and Future Secrets of Human Development. From the Contents of the Esoteric School
CW 93a Fundamentals of Esotericism
CW 94 Cosmogony. Popular Occultism. The Gospel of John. Theosophy Based on the Gospel of John
CW 95 At the Gates of Theosophy
CW 96 Origin-Impulses of Spiritual Science. Christian Esotericism in the Light of New Spirit-knowledge
CW 97 The Christian Mystery
CW 98 *Nature Beings and Spirit Beings: Their Activity in Our Visible World*
CW 99 The Theosophy of the Rosicrucians
CW 100 *True Knowledge of the Christ: Theosophy and Rosicucianism—The Gospel of John*
CW 101 Myths and Legends. Occult Signs and Symbols
CW 102 *Good and Evil Spirits and Their Influence on Humanity*
CW 103 *The Gospel of John*
CW 104 The Apocalypse of John
CW 104a From the Picture-Script of the Apocalypse of John
CW 105 *Universe, Earth, Human Being: Their Relationship to Egyptian Myths and Modern Civilization*
CW 106 Egyptian Myths and Mysteries in Relation to the Active Spiritual Forces of the Present
CW 107 *Disease, Karma, and Healing: Spiritual-scientific Enquiries into the Nature of the Human Being*

CW 108 Answering the Questions of Life and the World through Anthroposophy
CW 109 The Principle of Spiritual Economy in Connection with the Question of Reincarnation. An Aspect of the Spiritual Guidance of Humanity
CW 110 *The Spiritual Hierarchies and the Physical World: Zodiac, Planets, and Cosmos*
CW 111 Introduction to the Foundations of Theosophy
CW 112 The Gospel of John in Relation to the Three Other Gospels, Especially the Gospel of Luke
CW 113 The Orient in the Light of the Occident. The Children of Lucifer and the Brothers of Christ
CW 114 The Gospel of Luke
CW 115 Anthroposophy – Psychosophy – Pneumatosophy
CW 116 *The Christ-Impulse and the Development of Ego-Consciousness*
CW 117 *Deeper Secrets of Human Evolution in Light of the Gospels*
CW 117a The Gospel of John and the Three Other Gospels
CW 118 The Event of the Christ-Appearance in the Etheric World
CW 119 *Macrocosm and Microcosm: The Greater and the Lesser World: Questions Concerning the Soul, Life and the Spirit*
CW 120 The Revelations of Karma
CW 121 *The Mission of Folk Souls*
CW 122 The Secrets of the Biblical Creation-Story. The Six-Day Work in the First Book of Moses
CW 123 The Gospel of Matthew
CW 124 *Background to the Gospel of St Mark*
CW 125 *Paths and Goals of the Spiritual Human Being: Life Questions in the Light of Spiritual Science*
CW 126 Occult History. Esoteric Observations of the Karmic Relationships of Personalities and Events of World History
CW 127 *The Mission of the New Spiritual Revelation: The Pivotal Nature of the Christ Event in Earth Evolution*
CW 128 An Occult Physiology
CW 129 *Wonders of the World: Trials of the Soul, Revelations of the Spirit*
CW 130 Esoteric Christianity and the Spiritual Guidance of Humanity
CW 131 From Jesus to Christ
CW 132 *Inner Experiences of Evolution*
CW 133 The Earthly and the Cosmic Human Being
CW 134 *The World of the Senses and the World of the Spirit*
CW 135 Reincarnation and Karma and Their Meaning for the Culture of the Present
CW 136 *Spiritual Beings in the Heavenly Bodies and in the Kingdoms of Nature*
CW 137 The Human Being in the Light of Occultism, Theosophy and Philosophy
CW 138 On Initiation. On Eternity and the Passing Moment. On the Light of the Spirit and the Darkness of Life

CW 139	The Gospel of Mark
CW 140	Occult Investigation into the Life between Death and New Birth. The Living Interaction between Life and Death
CW 141	*Between Death and Rebirth: In Relation to Cosmic Facts*
CW 142/46	*The Bhagavad Gita and the West: The Esoteric Significance of the Bhagavad Gita and Its Relation to the Epistles of Paul*
CW 143	*Three Paths to Christ: Experiencing the Supersensible*
CW 144	*The Mysteries of Initiation: From Isis to the Holy Grail*
CW 145	What Significance Does Occult Development of the Human Being Have for the Sheaths–Physical Body, Etheric Body, Astral Body, and Self?
CW 146	[See CW 142/46]
CW 147	The Secrets of the Threshold
CW 148	The Fifth Gospel
CW 149	*Christ and the Spiritual World: The Quest for the Holy Grail*
CW 150	*How the Spiritual World Projects into Physical Existence: The Influence of the Dead*
CW 151	*Human and Cosmic Thought*
CW 152	*Approaching the Mystery of Golgotha*
CW 153	The Inner Being of Man and Life Between Death and New Birth
CW 154	How Does One Gain an Understanding of the Spiritual World? The Flowing in of Spiritual Impulses from out of the World of the Deceased
CW 155	*Christ and the Human Soul: The Meaning of Life – The Spiritual Foundation of Morality – Anthroposophy and Christianity*
CW 156	*Inner Reading and Inner Hearing: And How to Achieve Existence in the World of Ideas*
CW 157	Human Destinies and the Destiny of Peoples
CW 157a	The Formation of Destiny and the Life after Death
CW 158	*Our Connection with the Elemental World: Kalevala – Olaf Åsteson – the Russian People: The World as the Result of Balancing Influences*
CW 159	*The Mystery of Death: The Nature and Significance of Central Europe and the European Folk-Spirits*
CW 160	[Blank number]
CW 161	*Artistic Sensitivity as a Spiritual Approach to Knowing Life and the World*
CW 162	Questions of Art and Life in Light of Spiritual Science
CW 163	Coincidence, Necessity and Providence. Imaginative Knowledge and the Processes after Death
CW 164	*The Value of Thinking for a Cognition that Satisfies the Human Being: The Relationship between Spiritual Science and Natural Science*
CW 165	*Unifying Humanity Spiritually through the Christ Impulse*
CW 166	Necessity and Freedom in World Events and in Human Action
CW 167	*The Human Spirit Past and Present: Occult Fraternities and the Mystery of Golgotha*
CW 168	*The Connection between the Living and the Dead*
CW 169	World-being and Selfhood

CW 170 The Riddle of the Human Being. The Spiritual Background of Human History
CW 171 Inner Development-Impulses of Humanity. Goethe and the Crisis of the 19th Century.
CW 172 The Karma of the Vocation of the Human Being in Connection with Goethe's Life.
CW 173a Observations of Modern History, Vol. I: Paths to an Objective Judgment;
CW 173b Observations of Modern History, Vol. II: The Karma of Untruthfulness
CW 173c Observations of Modern History, Vol. III: The Reality of Occult Impulses
CW 174a *Europe Between East and West in Cosmic and Human History*
CW 174b *The Spiritual Background to the First World War*
CW 175 *Building Stones for an Understanding of the Mystery of Golgotha: Human Life in a Cosmic Context*
CW 176 *The Karma of Materialism: Aspects of Human Evolution*
CW 177 *The Fall of the Spirits of Darkness: The Spiritual Background to the Outer World: Spiritual Beings and Their Effects*
CW 178 Individual Spiritual Beings and Their Influence in the Soul of the Human Being
CW 179 *The Influence of the Dead on Destiny*
CW 180 Mystery Truths and Christmas Impulses. Ancient Myths and their Meaning.
CW 181 *Dying Earth and Living Cosmos: The Living Gifts of Anthroposophy: The Need for New Forms of Consciousness*
CW 182 Death as Transformation of Life
CW 183 *Human Evolution: A Spiritual-Scientific Quest*
CW 184 *Eternal and Transient Elements in Human Life: The Cosmic Past of Humanity and the Mystery of Evil*
CW 185 Historical Symptomology
CW 185a Historical-Developmental Foundations for Forming a Social Judgment
CW 186 The Fundamental Social Demands of Our Time. In Changed Times
CW 187 How Can Humanity Find the Christ Again? The Threefold Shadow-Existence of our Time and the New Christ-Light
CW 188 Goetheanism, a Transformation-Impulse and Resurrection-Thought. Science of the Human Being and Science of Sociology
CW 189 *Conscious Society: Anthroposophy and the Social Question*
CW 190 *Past and Future Impulses in Societal Events*
CW 191 *Understanding Society through Spiritual-Scientific Knowledge: Social Threefolding, Christ, Lucifer, and Ahriman*
CW 192 Spiritual-Scientific Treatment of Social and Pedagogical Questions
CW 193 *Problems of Society: An Esoteric View, from Luciferic Past to Ahrimanic Future*

CW 194 *Michael's Mission: Revealing the Essential Secrets of Human Nature*
CW 195 *Cosmic New Year: Thoughts for New Year 1920*
CW 196 *What Is Necessary in These Urgent Times*
CW 197 *Polarities in the Evolution of Humanity: West and East – Materialism and Mysticism – Knowledge and Belief*
CW 198 Healing Factors for the Social Organism
CW 199 Spiritual Science as Knowledge of the Foundational Impulses of Social Formation
CW 200 The New Spirituality and the Christ-Experience of the 20th Century
CW 201 The Correspondences Between Microcosm and Macrocosm. The Human Being – A Hieroglyph of the Universe.
CW 202 *Universal Spirituality and Human Physicality: Bridging the Divide: The Search for the New Isis and the Divine Sophia*
CW 203 The Responsibility of Human Beings for the Development of the World through their Spiritual Connection with the Planet Earth and the World of the Stars.
CW 204 Perspectives of the Development of Humanity. The Materialistic Knowledge-Impulse and the Task of Anthroposophy.
CW 205 Human Development, World-Soul, and World-Spirit. Part One: The Human Being as a Being of Body and Soul in Relationship to the World.
CW 206 Human Development, World-Soul, and World-Spirit. Part Two: The Human Being as a Spiritual Being in the Process of Historical Development
CW 207 Anthroposophy as Cosmosophy. Part One: Characteristic Features of the Human Being in the Earthly and the Cosmic Realms
CW 208 Anthroposophy as Cosmosophy. Part Two: The Forming of the Human Being as the Result of Cosmic Influence
CW 209 *The Language of the Cosmos: Cosmic Influences and the Spiritual Task of Northern Europe*
CW 210 Old and New Methods of Initiation. Drama and Poetry in the Change of Consciousness in the Modern Age
CW 211 *The Sun Mystery and the Mystery of Death and Resurrection: Exoteric and Esoteric Christianity*
CW 212 *Life of the Human Soul: And Its Relation to World Evolution*
CW 213 Human Questions and World Answers
CW 214 The Mystery of the Trinity: The Human Being in Relationship with the Spiritual World in the Course of Time
CW 215 Philosophy, Cosmology, and Religion in Anthroposophy
CW 216 *Supersensible Impulses in the Historical Development of Humanity*
CW 217 *Becoming the Archangel Michael's Companions: Rudolf Steiner's Challenge to the Younger Generation*
CW 217a *Youth and the Etheric Heart: Rudolf Steiner Speaks to the Younger Generation*
CW 218 *Spirit as Sculptor of the Human Organism*

CW 219 The Relationship of the World of the Stars to the Human Being, and of the Human Being to the World of the Stars. The Spiritual Communion of Humanity

CW 220 *Awake! For the Sake of the Future*

CW 221 Earth-Knowing and Heaven-Insight

CW 222 *The Driving Force of Spiritual Powers in World History*

CW 223 The Cycle of the Year as Breathing Process of the Earth and the Four Great Festival-Seasons. Anthroposophy and the Human Heart (*Gemüt*)

CW 224 The Human Soul and its Connection with Divine-Spiritual Individualities. The Internalization of the Festivals of the Year

CW 225 *Three Perspectives of Anthroposophy: Cultural Phenomena from the Point of View of Spiritual Science*

CW 226 Human Being, Human Destiny, and World Development

CW 227 Initiation-Knowledge

CW 228 *Initiation Science: And the Development of the Human Mind*

CW 229 The Experiencing of the Course of the Year in Four Cosmic Imaginations

CW 230 The Human Being as Harmony of the Creative, Building, and Formative World-Word

CW 231 The Supersensible Human Being, Understood Anthroposophically

CW 232 The Forming of the Mysteries

CW 233 *World History and the Mysteries in the Light of Anthroposophy*

CW 233a *Rosicrucianism and Modern Initiation: Mystery Centres of the Middle Ages: The Easter Festival and the History of the Mysteries*

CW 234 Anthroposophy. A Summary after 21 Years

CW 235 Esoteric Observations of Karmic Relationships in 6 Volumes, Vol. 1

CW 236 Esoteric Observations of Karmic Relationships in 6 Volumes, Vol. 2

CW 237 Esoteric Observations of Karmic Relationships in 6 Volumes, Vol. 3: The Karmic Relationships of the Anthroposophical Movement

CW 238 Esoteric Observations of Karmic Relationships in 6 Volumes, Vol. 4: The Spiritual Life of the Present in Relationship to the Anthroposophical Movement

CW 239 Esoteric Observations of Karmic Relationships in 6 Volumes, Vol. 5

CW 240 Esoteric Observations of Karmic Relationships in 6 Volumes, Vol. 6

CW 241 [Blank number]

CW 242 [Blank number]

CW 243 *True and False Paths of Spiritual Research*

CW 244 Answers to Questions, and Interviews

CW 245 [Blank number]

CW 246 Supplementary Volume I: Individual Members Lectures

CW 247 Supplementary Volume II: Individual Members Lectures

CW 248 [Blank number]

CW 249 [Blank number]

CW 250 On the History of the German Section of the Theosophical Society 1902–1913. Lectures, Speeches, Reports, and Minutes

CW 251 On the History of the Anthroposophical Society 1913–1922
CW 252 On the History of the Building Association and the Goetheanum Association 1911–1924
CW 253 *Sexuality, Inner Development, and Community Life: Ethical and Spiritual Dimensions of the Crisis in the Anthroposophical Society in Dornach, 1915*
CW 254 The Occult Movement in the 19th Century and Its Relationship to World Culture. Significant Points from the Exoteric Cultural Life around the Middle of the 19th Century
CW 255b Anthroposophy and Its Opponents
CW 256 [Blank number]
CW 257 Anthroposophical Community-Building
CW 258 *The Anthroposophic Movement: The History and Conditions of the Anthroposophical Movement in Relation to the Anthroposophical Society: An Encouragement for Self-Examination*
CW 259 The Year of Destiny 1923 in the History of the Anthroposophical Society. From the Burning of the Goetheanum to the Christmas Conference
CW 260 The Christmas Conference for the Founding of the General Anthroposophical Society 1923/24
CW 260a The Constitution of the General Anthroposophical Society and the School for Spiritual Science. The Rebuilding of the Goetheanum
CW 261 *Our Dead: Memorial, Funeral, and Cremation Addresses 1906–1924*
CW 262 Rudolf Steiner and Marie Steiner-von Sivers: Correspondence and Documents, 1901–1925
CW 263/1 Rudolf Steiner and Edith Maryon: Correspondence: Letters, Verses, Sketches, 1912–1924
CW 264 *From the History and Contents of the First Section of the Esoteric School: Letters, Documents, and Lectures: 1904–1914*
CW 265 *Freemasonry and Ritual Work: The Misraim Service*
CW 265a Teaching and Instruction Lessons for Members of the Knowledge-Cultic Section of the Esoteric School 1904–1914 [forthcoming]
CW 266/1 *From the Esoteric School: Esoteric Lessons 1904–1909*
CW 266/2 *From the Esoteric School: Esoteric Lessons 1910–1912*
CW 266/3 *From the Esoteric School: Esoteric Lessons 1913–1923*
CW 267 *Soul Exercises: Word and Symbol Meditations*
CW 268 *Mantric Sayings: Meditations 1903–1925*
CW 269 Ritual Texts for the Celebration of the Free Christian Religious Instruction. The Collected Verses for Teachers and Students of the Waldorf School
CW 270 Esoteric Instructions for the First Class of the School for Spiritual Science at the Goetheanum 1924, 4 Volumes

III. Lectures and Courses on Specific Realms of Life

Lectures on Art

CW 271 *Art and Theory of Art: Foundations of a New Aesthetics*
CW 272 *Anthroposophy in the Light of Goethe's* Faust*: Volume One of Spiritual-Scientific Commentaries on Goethe's* Faust
CW 273 *Goethe's* Faust *in the Light of Anthroposophy: Volume Two of Spiritual-Scientific Commentaries on Goethe's* Faust
CW 274 Addresses for the Christmas Plays from the Old Folk Traditions
CW 275 Art in the Light of Mystery Wisdom
CW 276 *The Arts and Their Mission*
CW 277a The Origin and Development of Eurythmy 1912–1918
CW 277b The Origin and Development of Eurythmy 1918–1920
CW 277c The Origin and Development of Eurythmy 1920–1922 [forthcoming]
CW 277d The Origin and Development of Eurythmy 1923–1924 [forthcoming]
CW 278 Eurythmy as Visible Song
CW 279 *Eurythmy as Speech Made Visible: Speech Eurythmy Course*
CW 280 The Method and Nature of Speech Formation
CW 281 The Art of Recitation and Declamation
CW 282 Speech Formation and Dramatic Art
CW 283 The Nature of the Musical Element and the Experience of Tone in the Human Being
CW 284 *Rosicrucianism Renewed: The Unity of Art, Science & Religion: The Theosophical Congress of Whitsun 1907*
CW 285 [Blank number]
CW 286 Paths to a New Style of Architecture. 'And the Building Becomes Man'
CW 287 *Architecture as Peacework: The First Goetheanum, Dornach, 1914*
CW 288 *Architecture, Sculpture, and Painting of the First Goetheanum*
CW 289 The Building-Idea of the Goetheanum: Lectures with Slides from the Years 1920–1921
CW 290 *Toward a New Theory of Architecture: The First Goetheanum in Pictures* [no longer in the German GA]
CW 291 The Being of Colours
CW 291a Knowledge of Colours. Supplementary Volume to 'The Being of Colours'
CW 292 *Art History as a Reflection of Inner Spiritual Impulses*

Lectures on Education

CW 293 General Knowledge of the Human Being as the Foundation of Pedagogy
CW 294 The Art of Education: Methodology and Didactics

CW 295 The Art of Education: Seminar Discussions and Lectures on Lesson Planning
CW 296 The Question of Education as a Social Question
CW 297 The Idea and Practice of the Waldorf School
CW 297a Education for Life: Self-Education and the Practice of Pedagogy
CW 298 Rudolf Steiner in the Waldorf School
CW 299 Spiritual-Scientific Observations on Speech
CW 300a Conferences with the Teachers of the Free Waldorf School in Stuttgart, 1919 to 1924, in 3 Volumes, Vol. 1
CW 300b Conferences with the Teachers of the Free Waldorf School in Stuttgart, 1919 to 1924, in 3 Volumes, Vol. 2
CW 300c Conferences with the Teachers of the Free Waldorf School in Stuttgart, 1919 to 1924, in 3 Volumes, Vol. 3
CW 301 The Renewal of Pedagogical-Didactical Art through Spiritual Science
CW 302 Knowledge of the Human Being and the Forming of Class Lessons
CW 302a Education and Teaching from a Knowledge of the Human Being
CW 303 The Healthy Development of the Human Being
CW 304 Methods of Education and Teaching Based on Anthroposophy
CW 304a Anthroposophical Knowledge of the Human Being and Pedagogy
CW 305 The Soul-Spiritual Foundational Forces of the Art of Education Spiritual Values in Education and Social Life
CW 306 Pedagogical Praxis from the Viewpoint of a Spiritual-Scientific Knowledge of the Human Being. The Education of the Child and Young Human Beings
CW 307 The Spiritual Life of the Present and Education
CW 308 The Method of Teaching and the Life-Requirements for Teaching
CW 309 Anthroposophical Pedagogy and Its Prerequisites
CW 310 The Pedagogical Value of a Knowledge of the Human Being and the Cultural Value of Pedagogy
CW 311 The Art of Education from an Understanding of the Being of Humanity

Lectures on Medicine

CW 312 *Introducing Anthroposophical Medicine*
CW 313 *Illness and Therapy: Spiritual-Scientific Aspects of Healing*
CW 314 *Physiology and Healing: Treatment, Therapy, and Hygiene*
CW 315 Curative Eurythmy
CW 316 *Understanding Healing: Meditative Reflections on Deepening Medicine through Spiritual Science*
CW 317 *Education for Special Needs: The Curative Education Course*
CW 318 The Working Together of Doctors and Pastors
CW 319 *The Healing Process: Spirit, Nature & Our Bodies*

Lectures on Natural Science

CW 320 Spiritual-Scientific Impulses for the Development of Physics 1: The First Natural-Scientific Course: Light, Colour, Tone, Mass, Electricity, Magnetism
CW 321 Spiritual-Scientific Impulses for the Development of Physics 2: The Second Natural-Scientific Course: Warmth at the Border of Positive and Negative Materiality
CW 322 The Borders of the Knowledge of Nature
CW 323 *Interdisciplinary Astronomy: Third Scientific Course*
CW 324 Nature Observation, Mathematics, and Scientific Experimentation and Results from the Viewpoint of Anthroposophy
CW 324a The Fourth Dimension in Mathematics and Reality
CW 325 Natural Science and the World-Historical Development of Humanity since Ancient Times
CW 326 The Moment of the Coming Into Being of Natural Science in World History and Its Development Since Then
CW 327 Spiritual-Scientific Foundations for Success in Farming. The Agricultural Course

Lectures on Social Life and the Threefold Arrangement of the Social Organism

CW 328 The Social Question
CW 329 The Liberation of the Human Being as the Foundation for a New Social Form
CW 330 The Renewal of the Social Organism
CW 331 Work-Council and Socialization
CW 332a The Social Future
CW 332b Lectures and Speeches on Social and Economic Issues
CW 333 *Freedom of Thought and Societal Forces: Implementing the Demands of Modern Society*
CW 334 From the Unified State to the Threefold Social Organism
CW 335 The Crisis of the Present and the Path to Healthy Thinking
CW 336 The Great Questions of the Times and Anthroposophical Spiritual Knowledge
CW 337a Social Ideas, Social Realities, Social Practice, Vol. 1: Question-and-Answer Evenings and Study Evenings of the Alliance for the Threefold Social Organism in Stuttgart, 1919–1920
CW 337b Social Ideas, Social Realities, Social Practice, Vol. 2: Discussion Evenings of the Swiss Alliance for the Threefold Social Organism
CW 338 *Communicating Anthroposophy: The Course for Speakers to Promote the Idea of Threefolding*
CW 339 Anthroposophy, Threefold Social Organism, and the Art of Public Speaking
CW 340/41 *Rethinking Economics: Lectures and Seminars on World Economics*

Lectures and Courses on Christian Religious Work

CW 342 *First Steps in Christian Religious Renewal: Preparing the Ground for The Christian Community*
CW 343 Lectures and Courses on Christian Religious Work, Vol. 2: Spiritual Knowledge – Religious Feeling – Cultic Doing
CW 344 Lectures and Courses on Christian Religious Work, Vol. 3: Lectures at the Founding of The Christian Community
CW 345 Lectures and Courses on Christian Religious Work, Vol. 4: Concerning the Nature of the Working Word
CW 346 Lectures and Courses on Christian Religious Work, Vol. 5: The Apocalypse and the Work of the Priest

Lectures for Workers at the Goetheanum

CW 347 The Knowledge of the Nature of the Human Being According to Body, Soul and Spirit. On Earlier Conditions of the Earth
CW 348 On Health and Illness. Foundations of a Spiritual-Scientific Doctrine of the Senses
CW 349 On the Life of the Human Being and of the Earth. On the Nature of Christianity
CW 350 Rhythms in the Cosmos and in the Human Being. How Does One Come To See the Spiritual World?
CW 351 The Human Being and the World. The Influence of the Spirit in Nature. On the Nature of Bees
CW 352 Nature and the Human Being Observed Spiritual-Scientifically
CW 353 The History of Humanity and the World-Views of the Folk Cultures
CW 354 The Creation of the World and the Human Being. Life on Earth and the Influence of the Stars

C. Artistic Works

CW A 1–10; 57 The Architectural Work I: The Goetheanum and Its Predecessors
CW A 11 The Sculptural Work
CW A 12 The Goetheanum Windows. The Speech of Light. Sketches and Studies
CW A 13–16; 52–56 Painting Work
CW A 14 Sketches for the Painting of the Small Dome of the First Goetheanum
CW A 27–43 The Architectural Work II: Commercial and Residential Buildings in Dornach and Other Places [forthcoming]
CW A 45 The Graphic Work
CW A 48 The Drawing Work
CW A 51 The Art of Jewellery as a Goethean Language of Form

CW A 54.0 A Path of Training in Painting. Pastel Sketches and Watercolours
CW A 54.1 Nature Moods. Nine Training Sketches for Painters

Eurythmy Figures

CW A 26 Skectches of the Eurythmy Figures
CW A 26a The Eurythmy Figures of Rudolf Steiner, Artistically Executed by Annemarie Bäschlin
CW A 26b Eurythmy Figures from the Time When They Were Created

Eurythmy Forms

CW A 23/1 Volume I: Eurythmy Forms for Poems by Rudolf Steiner
CW A 23/2 Volume II: Eurythmy Forms for the Calendar of the Soul by Rudolf Steiner
CW A 23/3 Volume III: Euythmy Forms for Poems by J. W. von Goethe
CW A 23/4 Volume IV: Eurythmy Forms for Poems by Christian Morgenstern
CW A 23/5 Volume V: Eurythmy Forms for Poems by Albert Steffen
CW A 23/6 Volume VI: Eurythmy Forms for German Poems by Fercher von Steinwand, Hamerling, Hebbel, C. F. Meyer, Nietzsche, among others
CW A 23/7 Volume VII: Eurythmy Forms for English Poems
CW A 23/8 Volume VIII: Eurythmy Forms for French and Russian Poems
CW A 24 Volume IX: Eurythmy Forms for Tone Eurythmy

Blackboard Drawings from Lectures

CW A 58/1 Volume I: 20 Plates from Public Lectures 1920–1924 in CWs 73a, 74, 76, and 84
CW A 58/2 Volume II: 38 Plates from Lectures in 1919 in CWs 191 and 194
CW A 58/3 Volume III: 34 Plates from Lectures in 1920 in CWs 196 and 198
CW A 58/4 Volume IV: 33 Plates from Lectures in 1920 in CWs 199 and 200
CW A 58/5 Volume V: 31 Plates from Lectures in 1920 in CW 201
CW A 58/6 Volume VI: 46 Plates from Lectures 1920–1921 in CWs 202–204
CW A 58/7 Volume VII: 38 Plates from Lectures in 1921 in CWs 205 and 206
CW A 58/8 Volume VIII: 42 Plates from Lectures in 1921 in CWs 207–209
CW A 58/9 Volume IX: 40 Plates from Lectures in 1922 in CWs 210–212
CW A 58/10 Volume X: 35 Plates from Lectures in 1922 in CWs 213–215
CW A 58/11 Volume XI: 41 Plates from Lectures 1922–1923 in CWs 216, 218–220
CW A 58/12 Volume XII: 37 Plates from Lectures in 1923 in CWs 221–225
CW A 58/13 Volume XIII: 38 Plates from Lectures in 1923 in CWs 227–230
CW A 58/14 Volume XIV: 36 Plates from Lectures in 1923 in CWs 232 and 233
CW A 58/15 Volume XV: 37 Plates from Lectures in 1924 in CWs 233a, 234, and 243
CW A 58/16 Volume XVI: 56 Plates from the 'Karma Lectures' in CWs 235–238 and 240

CW A 58/17 Volume XVII: 21 Plates from Lectures on the History of the Anthroposophical Society in CWs 257, 258, 260, and 260a
CW A 58/18 Volume XVIII: 33 Plates from Lectures on Art in CWs 271, 276, 283, 288–290, and 291
CW A 58/19 Volume XIX: 41 Plates from Lectures on Eurythmy in CWs 278, 279, and 315
CW A 58/20 Volume XX: 27 Plates from Lectures on Speech Formation in CWs 281 and 282
CW A 58/21 Volume XXI: 42 Plates from Lectures on Education in CWs 296, 303, 304, 306, and 311
CW A 58/22 Volume XXII: 46 Plates from Lectures on Medicine in CWs 312–315
CW A 58/23 Volume XXIII: 48 Plates from Lectures in 1924 in CWs 316–318
CW A 58/24 Volume XXIV: 39 Plates from Lectures on Natural Science and the Social Question in CWs 322, 326, 327, 339, and 340
CW A 58/25 Volume XXV: 33 Plates from the 'Workers Lectures' (Volumes 1 and 2) in CWs 347 and 348
CW A 58/26 Volume XXVI: 51 Plates from the 'Workers Lectures' (Volumes 3 and 4) in CWs 349 and 350
CW A 58/27 Volume XXVII: 35 Plates from the 'Workers Lectures' (Volumes 5 and 6) in CWs 351 and 352
CW A 58/28 Volume XXVIII: 42 Plates from the 'Workers Lectures' (Volumes 7 and 8) in CWs 353 and 354
CW A 58/29 Volume XXIX: 43 Plates from Lectures and Courses on Christian Religious Activity in CWs 342–344 and 346
CW A 58/30 Volume XXX: 27 Plates from CWs 255b, 324a, 337b, and 340, Corrigenda, Plates without CW Assignment, Copies

SIGNIFICANT EVENTS IN THE LIFE OF RUDOLF STEINER

1829: June 23: birth of Johann Steiner (1829–1910)—Rudolf Steiner's father—in Geras, Lower Austria.

1834: May 8: birth of Franciska Blie (1834–1918)—Rudolf Steiner's mother—in Horn, Lower Austria. 'My father and mother were both children of the glorious Lower Austrian forest district north of the Danube.'

1860: May 16: marriage of Johann Steiner and Franciska Blie.

1861: February 25: birth of *Rudolf Joseph Lorenz Steiner* in Kraljevec, Croatia, near the border with Hungary, where Johann Steiner works as a telegrapher for the South Austria Railroad. Rudolf Steiner is baptized two days later, February 27, the date usually given as his birthday.

1862: Summer: the family moves to Modling, Lower Austria.

1863: The family moves to Pottschach, Lower Austria, near the Styrian border, where Johann Steiner becomes stationmaster. 'The view stretched to the mountains . . . majestic peaks in the distance and the sweet charm of nature in the immediate surroundings.'

1864: November 15: birth of Rudolf Steiner's sister, Leopoldine (d. November 1, 1927). She will become a seamstress and live with her parents for the rest of her life.

1866: July 28: birth of Rudolf Steiner's deaf-mute brother, Gustav (d. May 1, 1941).

1867: Rudolf Steiner enters the village school. Following a disagreement between his father and the schoolmaster, whose wife falsely accused the boy of causing a commotion, Rudolf Steiner is taken out of school and taught at home.

1868: A critical experience. Unknown to the family, an aunt dies in a distant town. Sitting in the station waiting room, Rudolf Steiner sees her 'form', which speaks to him, asking for help. 'Beginning with this experience, a new soul life began in the boy, one in which not only the outer trees and mountains spoke to him, but also the worlds that lay behind them. From this moment on, the boy began to live with the spirits of nature . . .'

1869: The family moves to the peaceful, rural village of Neudorfl, near Wiener Neustadt in present-day Austria. Rudolf Steiner attends the village school. Because of the 'unorthodoxy' of his writing and spelling, he has to do 'extra lessons'.

1870: Through a book lent to him by his tutor, he discovers geometry: 'To grasp something purely in the spirit brought me inner happiness. I know that I first learned happiness through geometry.' The same tutor allows him to draw, while other students still struggle with their reading and writing. 'An artistic element' thus enters his education.

1871: Though his parents are not religious, Rudolf Steiner becomes a 'church child', a favourite of the priest, who was 'an exceptional character'. 'Up to the age of ten or eleven, among those I came to know, he was far and away the most significant.' Among other things, he introduces Steiner to Copernican, heliocentric cosmology. As an altar boy, Rudolf Steiner serves at Masses, funerals, and Corpus Christi processions. At year's end, after an incident in which he escapes a thrashing, his father forbids him to go to church.

1872: Rudolf Steiner transfers to grammar school in Wiener-Neustadt, a five-mile walk from home, which must be done in all weathers.

1873–75: Through his teachers and on his own, Rudolf Steiner has many wonderful experiences with science and mathematics. Outside school, he teaches himself analytic geometry, trigonometry, differential equations, and calculus.

1876: Rudolf Steiner begins tutoring other students. He learns bookbinding from his father. He also teaches himself stenography.

1877: Rudolf Steiner discovers Kant's *Critique of Pure Reason,* which he reads and rereads. He also discovers and reads von Rotteck's *World History.*

1878: He studies extensively in contemporary psychology and philosophy.

1879: Rudolf Steiner graduates from high school with honours. His father is transferred to Inzersdorf, near Vienna. He uses his first visit to Vienna 'to purchase a great number of philosophy books'—Kant, Fichte, Schelling, and Hegel, as well as numerous histories of philosophy. His aim: to find a path from the 'I' to nature.

October 1879–1883: Rudolf Steiner attends the Technical College in Vienna—to study mathematics, chemistry, physics, mineralogy, botany, zoology, biology, geology, and mechanics—with a scholarship. He also attends lectures in history and literature, while avidly reading philosophy on his own. His two favourite professors are Karl Julius Schröer (German language and literature) and Edmund Reitlinger (physics). He also audits lectures by Robert Zimmermann on aesthetics and Franz Brentano on philosophy. During this year he begins his friendship with Moritz Zitter (1861–1921), who will help support him financially when he is in Berlin.

1880: Rudolf Steiner attends lectures on Schiller and Goethe by Karl Julius Schröer, who becomes his mentor. Also 'through a remarkable combination of circumstances', he meets Felix Koguzki, a 'herb gatherer' and healer, who could 'see deeply into the secrets of nature'. Rudolf Steiner will meet and study with this 'emissary of the Master' throughout his time in Vienna.

1881: January: '... I didn't sleep a wink. I was busy with philosophical problems until about 12:30 a.m. Then, finally, I threw myself down on my couch. All my striving during the previous year had been to research whether the following statement by Schelling was true or not: *Within everyone dwells a secret, marvellous capacity to draw back from the stream of time—out of the self clothed in all that comes to us from outside—into our innermost being and there, in the immutable form of the Eternal, to look into ourselves.* I believe, and I am still quite certain of it, that I discovered this capacity in myself; I had long had an inkling of it. Now the whole of idealist philosophy stood before me in modified form. What's a sleepless night compared to that!'

Rudolf Steiner begins communicating with leading thinkers of the day, who send him books in return, which he reads eagerly.

July: 'I am not one of those who dives into the day like an animal in human form. I pursue a quite specific goal, an idealistic aim—knowledge of the truth! This cannot be done offhandedly. It requires the greatest striving in the world, free of all egotism, and equally of all resignation.'

August: Steiner puts down on paper for the first time thoughts for a 'Philosophy of Freedom'. 'The striving for the absolute: this human yearning is freedom.' He also seeks to outline a 'peasant philosophy', describing what the worldview of a 'peasant'—one who lives close to the earth and the old ways—really is.

1881–1882: Felix Koguzki, the herb gatherer, reveals himself to be the envoy of another, higher initiatory personality, who instructs Rudolf Steiner to penetrate Fichte's philosophy and to master modern scientific thinking as a preparation for right entry into the spirit. This 'Master' also teaches him the double (evolutionary and involutionary) nature of time.

1882: Through the offices of Karl Julius Schröer, Rudolf Steiner is asked by Joseph Kürschner to edit Goethe's scientific works for the *Deutschen National-Literatur* edition. He writes 'A Possible Critique of Atomistic Concepts' and sends it to Friedrich Theodor Vischer.

1883: Rudolf Steiner completes his college studies and begins work on the Goethe project.

1884: First volume of Goethe's *Scientific Writings* (CW 1) appears (March). He lectures on Goethe and Lessing, and Goethe's approach to science. In July, he enters the household of Ladislaus and Pauline Specht as tutor to the four Specht boys. He will live there until 1890. At this time, he meets Josef Breuer (1842–1925), the co-author with Sigmund Freud of *Studies in Hysteria,* who is the Specht family doctor.

1885: While continuing to edit Goethe's writings, Rudolf Steiner reads deeply in contemporary philosophy (Eduard von Hartmann, Johannes Volkelt, and Richard Wahle, among others).

1886: May: Rudolf Steiner sends Kürschner the manuscript of *Outlines of Goethe's Theory of Knowledge* (CW 2), which appears in October, and which he sends out widely. He also meets the poet Marie Eugenie Delle Grazie and writes 'Nature and Our Ideals' for her. He attends her salon, where he meets many priests, theologians, and philosophers, who will become his friends. Meanwhile, the director of the Goethe Archive in Weimar requests his collaboration with the *Sophien* edition of Goethe's works, particularly the writings on colour.

1887: At the beginning of the year, Rudolf Steiner is very sick. As the year progresses and his health improves, he becomes increasingly 'a man of letters', lecturing, writing essays, and taking part in Austrian cultural life. In August–September, the second volume of Goethe's *Scientific Writings* appears.

1888: January–July: Rudolf Steiner assumes editorship of the 'German Weekly' *(Deutsche Wochenschrift)*. He begins lecturing more intensively, giving, for example, a lecture titled 'Goethe as Father of a New Aesthetics'. He meets and becomes soul friends with Friedrich Eckstein (1861–1939), a vegetarian, philosopher of symbolism, alchemist, and musician, who will introduce him to various spiritual currents (including Theosophy) and with whom he will meditate and interpret esoteric and alchemical texts.

1889: Rudolf Steiner first reads Nietzsche *(Beyond Good and Evil)*. He encounters Theosophy again and learns of Madame Blavatsky in the theosophical circle around Marie Lang (1858–1934). Here he also meets well-known figures of Austrian life, as well as esoteric figures like the occultist Franz Hartmann and Karl Leinigen-Billigen (translator of C.G. Harrison's *The Transcendental Universe)*. During this period, Steiner first reads A.P. Sinnett's *Esoteric Buddhism* and Mabel Collins's *Light on the Path*. He also begins travelling, visiting Budapest, Weimar, and Berlin (where he meets philosopher Eduard von Hartmann).

1890: Rudolf Steiner finishes Volume 3 of Goethe's scientific writings. He begins his doctoral dissertation, which will become *Truth and Science* (CW 3). He also meets the poet and feminist Rosa Mayreder

(1858–1938), with whom he can exchange his most intimate thoughts. In September, Rudolf Steiner moves to Weimar to work in the Goethe-Schiller Archive.

1891: Volume 3 of the Kürschner edition of Goethe appears. Meanwhile, Rudolf Steiner edits Goethe's studies in mineralogy and scientific writings for the *Sophien* edition. He meets Ludwig Laistner of the Cotta Publishing Company, who asks for a book on the basic question of metaphysics. From this will result, ultimately, *The Philosophy of Freedom* (CW 4), which will be published not by Cotta but by Emil Felber. In October, Rudolf Steiner takes the oral exam for a doctorate in philosophy, mathematics, and mechanics at Rostock University, receiving his doctorate on the twenty-sixth. In November, he gives his first lecture on Goethe's 'Fairy Tale' in Vienna.

1892: Rudolf Steiner continues work at the Goethe-Schiller Archive and on his *Philosophy of Freedom. Truth and Science,* his doctoral dissertation, is published. Steiner undertakes to write Introductions to books on Schopenhauer and Jean Paul for Cotta. At year's end, he finds lodging with Anna Eunike, née Schulz (1853–1911), a widow with four daughters and a son. He also develops a friendship with Otto Erich Hartleben (1864–1905) with whom he shares literary interests.

1893: Rudolf Steiner begins his habit of producing many reviews and articles. In March, he gives a lecture titled 'Hypnotism, with Reference to Spiritism'. In September, volume 4 of the Kürschner edition is completed. In November, *The Philosophy of Freedom* appears. This year, too, he meets John Henry Mackay (1864–1933), the anarchist, and Max Stirner, a scholar and biographer.

1894: Rudolf Steiner meets Elisabeth Fürster Nietzsche, the philosopher's sister, and begins to read Nietzsche in earnest, beginning with the as yet unpublished *Antichrist.* He also meets Ernst Haeckel (1834–1919). In the fall, he begins to write *Nietzsche, A Fighter against His Time* (CW 5).

1895: May, *Nietzsche, A Fighter against His Time* appears.

1896: January 22: Rudolf Steiner sees Friedrich Nietzsche for the first and only time. Moves between the Nietzsche and the Goethe-Schiller Archives, where he completes his work before year's end. He falls out with Elisabeth Förster Nietzsche, thus ending his association with the Nietzsche Archive.

1897: Rudolf Steiner finishes the manuscript of *Goethe's Worldview* (CW 6). He moves to Berlin with Anna Eunike and begins editorship of the *Magazin fiir Literatur.* From now on, Steiner will write countless reviews, literary and philosophical articles, and so on. He begins lecturing at the 'Free Literary Society'. In September, he attends the Zionist Congress in Basel. He sides with Dreyfus in the Dreyfus affair.

1898: Rudolf Steiner is very active as an editor in the political, artistic, and theatrical life of Berlin. He becomes friendly with John Henry Mackay and poet Ludwig Jacobowski (1868–1900). He joins Jacobowski's circle of writers, artists, and scientists—'The Coming Ones' (*Die Kommenden*)—and contributes lectures to the group until 1903. He also lectures at the 'League for College Pedagogy'. He writes an article for Goethe's sesquicentennial, 'Goethe's Secret Revelation', on the 'Fairy Tale of the Green Snake and the Beautiful Lily'.

1898–99: 'This was a trying time for my soul as I looked at Christianity. . . . I was able to progress only by contemplating, by means of spiritual perception, the evolution of Christianity. . . . Conscious knowledge of real Christianity began to dawn in me around the turn of the century. This seed continued to develop. My soul trial occurred shortly before the beginning of the twentieth century. It was decisive for my soul's development that I stood spiritually before the Mystery of Golgotha in a deep and solemn celebration of knowledge.'

1899: Rudolf Steiner begins teaching and giving lectures and lecture cycles at the Workers' College, founded by Wilhelm Liebknecht (1826–1900). He will continue to do so until 1904. Writes: *Literature and Spiritual Life in the Nineteenth Century; Individualism in Philosophy; Haeckel and His Opponents; Poetry in the Present;* and begins what will become (fifteen years later) *The Riddles of Philosophy* (CW 18). He also meets many artists and writers, including Käthe Kollwitz, Stefan Zweig, and Rainer Maria Rilke. On October 31, he marries Anna Eunike.

1900: 'I thought that the turn of the century must bring humanity a new light. It seemed to me that the separation of human thinking and willing from the spirit had peaked. A turn or reversal of direction in human evolution seemed to me a necessity.' Rudolf Steiner finishes *World and Life Views in the Nineteenth Century* (the second part of what will become *The Riddles of Philosophy)* and dedicates it to Ernst Haeckel. It is published in March. He continues lecturing at *Die Kommenden,* whose leadership he assumes after the death of Jacobowski. Also, he gives the Gutenberg Jubilee lecture before 7,000 typesetters and printers. In September, Rudolf Steiner is invited by Count and Countess Brockdorff to lecture in the Theosophical Library. His first lecture is on Nietzsche. His second lecture is titled 'Goethe's Secret Revelation.' October 6, he begins a lecture cycle on the mystics that will become *Mystics after Modernism* (CW 7). November–December: 'Marie von Sivers appears in the audience. . . .' Also in November, Steiner gives his first lecture at the Giordano Bruno Bund (where he will continue to lecture until May, 1905). He speaks on Bruno and modern Rome, focusing on the importance of the philosophy of Thomas Aquinas as monism.

1901: In continual financial straits, Rudolf Steiner's early friends Moritz Zitter and Rosa Mayreder help support him. In October, he begins the lecture cycle *Christianity as Mystical Fact* (CW 8) at the Theosophical Library. In November, he gives his first 'theosophical lecture' on Goethe's 'Fairy Tale' in Hamburg at the invitation of Wilhelm Hubbe-Schleiden. He also attends a gathering to celebrate the founding of the Theosophical Society at Count and Countess Brockdorff's. He gives a lecture cycle, 'From Buddha to Christ,' for the circle of the *Kommenden*. November 17, Marie von Sivers asks Rudolf Steiner if Theosophy needs a Western–Christian spiritual movement (to complement Theosophy's Eastern emphasis). 'The question was posed. Now, following spiritual laws, I could begin to give an answer. . . .' In December, Rudolf Steiner writes his first article for a theosophical publication. At year's end, the Brockdorffs and possibly Wilhelm Hubbe-Schleiden ask Rudolf Steiner to join the Theosophical Society and undertake the leadership of the German section. Rudolf Steiner agrees, on the condition that Marie von Sivers (then in Italy) work with him.

1902: Beginning in January, Rudolf Steiner attends the opening of the Workers' School in Spandau with Rosa Luxemberg (1870–1919). January 17, Rudolf Steiner joins the Theosophical Society. In April, he is asked to become general secretary of the German Section of the Theosophical Society, and works on preparations for its founding. In July, he visits London for a theosophical congress. He meets Bertram Keightly, G.R.S. Mead, A.P. Sinnett, and Annie Besant, among others. In September, *Christianity as Mystical Fact* appears. In October, Rudolf Steiner gives his first public lecture on Theosophy ('Monism and Theosophy') to about three hundred people at the Giordano Bruno Bund. On October 19–21, the German Section of the Theosophical Society has its first meeting; Rudolf Steiner is the general secretary, and Annie Besant attends. Steiner lectures on practical karma studies. On October 23, Annie Besant inducts Rudolf Steiner into the Esoteric School of the Theosophical Society. On October 25, Steiner begins a weekly series of lectures: 'The Field of Theosophy'. During this year, Rudolf Steiner also first meets Ita Wegman (1876–1943), who will become his close collaborator in his final years.

1903: Rudolf Steiner holds about 300 lectures and seminars. In May, the first issue of the periodical *Luzifer* appears. In June, Rudolf Steiner visits London for the first meeting of the Federation of the European Sections of the Theosophical Society, where he meets Colonel Olcott. He begins to write *Theosophy* (CW 9).

1904: Rudolf Steiner continues lecturing at the Workers' College and elsewhere (about 90 lectures), while lecturing intensively all over Germany among theosophists (about 140 lectures). In February, he meets Carl Unger (1878–1929), who will become a member of the board of the Anthroposophical Society (1913). In March, he meets Michael Bauer (1871–1929), a Christian mystic, who will also be on the board. In May, *Theosophy* appears, with the dedication: 'To the spirit of Giordano Bruno'. Rudolf Steiner and Marie von Sivers visit London for meetings with Annie Besant. June: Rudolf Steiner and Marie von Sivers attend the meeting of the Federation of European Sections of the Theosophical Society in Amsterdam. In July, Steiner begins the articles in *Luzifer-Gnosis* that will become *How to Know Higher Worlds* (CW 10) and *Cosmic Memory* (CW 11). In September, Annie Besant visits Germany. In December, Steiner lectures on Freemasonry. He mentions the High Grade Masonry derived from John Yarker and represented by Theodore Reuss and Karl Kellner as a blank slate 'into which a good image could be placed'.

1905: This year, Steiner ends his non-theosophical lecturing activity. Supported by Marie von Sivers, his theosophical lecturing—both in public and in the Theosophical Society—increases significantly: 'The German Theosophical Movement is of exceptional importance.' Steiner recommends reading, among others, Fichte, Jacob Boehme, and Angelus Silesius. He begins to introduce Christian themes into Theosophy. He also begins to work with doctors (Felix Peipers and Ludwig Noll). In July, he is in London for the Federation of European Sections, where he attends a lecture by Annie Besant: 'I have seldom seen Mrs Besant speak in so inward and heartfelt a manner... Through Mrs Besant I have found the way to H.P. Blavatsky.' September to October, he gives a course of 31 lectures for a small group of esoteric students. In October, the annual meeting of the German Section of the Theosophical Society, which still remains very small, takes place. Rudolf Steiner reports membership has risen from 121 to 377 members. In November, seeking to establish esoteric 'continuity', Rudolf Steiner and Marie von Sivers participate in a 'Memphis-Misraim' Masonic ceremony. They pay 45 marks for membership. 'Yesterday, you saw how little remains of former esoteric institutions.' 'We are dealing only with a "framework" ... for the present, nothing lies behind it. The occult powers have completely withdrawn.'

1906: Expansion of theosophical work. Rudolf Steiner gives about 245 lectures, only 44 of which take place in Berlin. Cycles are given in Paris, Leipzig, Stuttgart, and Munich. Esoteric work also intensifies. Rudolf Steiner begins writing *An Outline of Esoteric Science* (CW 13).

In January, Rudolf Steiner receives permission (a patent) from the Great Orient of the Scottish A & A Thirty-Three Degree Rite of the Order of the Ancient Freemasons of the Memphis-Misraim Rite to direct a chapter under the name 'Mystica Aeterna.' This will become the 'Cognitive-Ritual Section' (also called 'Misraim Service') of the Esoteric School. (See: *Freemasonry and Ritual Work: The Misraim Service,* CW 265.) During this time, Steiner also meets Albert Schweitzer. In May, he is in Paris, where he visits Édouard Schuré. Many Russians attend his lectures (including Konstantin Balmont, Dimitri Mereszkovski, Zinaida Hippius, and Maximilian Woloshin). He attends the General Meeting of the European Federation of the Theosophical Society, at which Col Olcott is present for the last time. He spends the year's end in Venice and Rome, where he writes and works on his translation of H.P. Blavatsky's *Key to Theosophy.*

1907: Further expansion of the German Theosophical Movement according to the Rosicrucian directive to 'introduce spirit into the world'—in education, in social questions, in art, and in science. In February, Col Olcott dies in Adyar. Before he dies, Olcott indicates that 'the Masters' wish Annie Besant to succeed him: much politicking ensues. Rudolf Steiner supports Besant's candidacy. April–May: preparations for the Congress of the Federation of European Sections of the Theosophical Society—the great, watershed Whitsun 'Munich Congress,' attended by Annie Besant and others. Steiner decides to separate Eastern and Western (Christian–Rosicrucian) esoteric schools. He takes his esoteric school out of the Theosophical Society (Besant and Rudolf Steiner are 'in harmony' on this). Steiner makes his first lecture tours to Austria and Hungary. That summer, he is in Italy. In September, he visits Édouard Schuré, who will write the Introduction to the French edition of *Christianity as Mystical Fact* in Barr, Alsace. Rudolf Steiner writes the autobiographical statement known as the 'Barr Document.' In *Luzifer-Gnosis*, 'The Education of the Child' appears.

1908: The movement grows (membership: 1,150). Lecturing expands. Steiner makes his first extended lecture tour to Holland and Scandinavia, as well as visits to Naples and Sicily. Themes: St John's Gospel, the Apocalypse, Egypt, science, philosophy, and logic. *Luzifer-Gnosis* ceases publication. In Berlin, Marie von Sivers (with Johanna Mücke (1864–1949) forms the *Philosophisch-Theosophisch* (after 1915 *Philosophisch-Anthroposophisch) Verlag* to publish Steiner's work. Steiner gives lecture cycles titled *The Gospel of St John* (CW 103) and *The Apocalypse* (104).

1909: *An Outline of Esoteric Science* appears. Lecturing and travel continues. Rudolf Steiner's spiritual research expands to include the polarity of Lucifer and Ahriman; the work of great individualities in history; the Maitreya Buddha and the Bodhisattvas; spiritual economy (CW 109); the work of the spiritual hierarchies in heaven and on earth (CW 110). He also deepens and intensifies his research into the Gospels, giving lectures on the Gospel of St Luke (CW 114) with the first mention of two Jesus children. Meets and becomes friends with Christian Morgenstern (1871–1914). In April, he lays the foundation stone for the Malsch model—the building that will lead to the first Goetheanum. In May, the International Congress of the Federation of European Sections of the Theosophical Society takes place in Budapest. Rudolf Steiner receives the Subba Row medal for *How to Know Higher Worlds.* During this time, Charles W. Leadbeater discovers Jiddu Krishnamurti (1895–1986) and proclaims him the future 'world teacher,' the bearer of the Maitreya Buddha and the 'reappearing Christ.' In October, Steiner delivers seminal lectures on 'anthroposophy,' which he will try, unsuccessfully, to rework over the next years into the unfinished work, *Anthroposophy (A Fragment)* (CW 45).

1910: New themes: *The Reappearance of Christ in the Etheric* (CW 118); *The Fifth Gospel; The Mission of Folk Souls* (CW 121); *Occult History* (CW 126); the evolving development of etheric cognitive capacities. Rudolf Steiner continues his Gospel research with *The Gospel of St Matthew* (CW 123). In January, his father dies. In April, he takes a month-long trip to Italy, including Rome, Monte Cassino, and Sicily. He also visits Scandinavia again. July–August, he writes the first Mystery Drama, *The Portal of Initiation* (CW 14). In November, he gives 'psychosophy' lectures. In December, he submits 'On the Psychological Foundations and Epistemological Framework of Theosophy' to the International Philosophical Congress in Bologna.

1911: The crisis in the Theosophical Society deepens. In January, 'The Order of the Rising Sun,' which will soon become 'The Order of the Star in the East,' is founded for the coming world teacher, Krishnamurti. At the same time, Marie von Sivers, Rudolf Steiner's co-worker, falls ill. Fewer lectures are given, but important new ground is broken. In Prague, in March, Steiner meets Franz Kafka (1883–1924) and Hugo Bergmann (1883–1975). In April, he delivers his paper to the Philosophical Congress. He writes the second Mystery Drama, *The Soul's Probation* (CW 14). Also, while Marie von Sivers is convalescing, Rudolf Steiner begins work on *Calendar 1912/1913*, which will contain the 'Calendar of the Soul' meditations. On March 19, Anna (Eunike) Steiner dies. In September, Rudolf Steiner visits Einsiedeln, birthplace of Paracelsus. In December, Friedrich Rittelmeyer, future founder of The Christian Community, meets Rudolf Steiner. The *Johannes-Bauverein,* the 'building committee,' which would lead to the first Goetheanum (first planned for Munich), is also founded, and a preliminary committee for the founding of an independent association is created that, in the following year, will become the Anthroposophical Society. Important lecture cycles include *Occult Physiology* (CW 128); *Wonders of the World* (CW 129); *From Jesus to Christ* (CW 131). Other themes: esoteric Christianity; Christian Rosenkreutz; the spiritual guidance of humanity; the sense world and the world of the spirit.

1912: Despite the ongoing, now increasing crisis in the Theosophical Society, much is accomplished: *Calendar 1912/1913* is published; eurythmy is created; both the third Mystery Drama, *The Guardian of the Threshold* (CW 14) and *A Way of Self-Knowledge* (CW 16) are written. New (or renewed) themes included life between death and rebirth and karma and reincarnation. Other lecture cycles: *Spiritual Beings in the Heavenly Bodies and in the Kingdoms of Nature* (CW 136); *The Human Being in the Light of Occultism, Theosophy, and Philosophy* (CW 137); *The Gospel of St Mark* (CW 139); and *The Bhagavad Gita and the Epistles of Paul* (CW 142). On May 8, Rudolf Steiner celebrates White Lotus Day, H.P. Blavatsky's death day, which he had faithfully observed for the past decade, for the last time. In August, Rudolf Steiner suggests the 'independent association' be called the 'Anthroposophical Society.' In September, the first eurythmy course takes place. In October, Rudolf Steiner declines recognition of a Theosophical Society lodge dedicated to the Star of the East and decides to expel all Theosophical Society members belonging to the order. Also, with Marie von Sivers, he first visits Dornach, near Basel, Switzerland, and they stand on the hill where the Goetheanum will be built. In November, a Theosophical Society lodge is opened by direct mandate from Adyar (Annie Besant). In December, a meeting of the German section occurs at which it is decided that belonging to the Order of the Star of the East is incompatible with membership in the Theosophical Society. December 28: informal founding of the Anthroposophical Society in Berlin.

1913: Expulsion of the German section from the Theosophical Society. February 2–3: Foundation meeting of the Anthroposophical Society. Board members include: Marie von Sivers, Michael Bauer, and Carl Unger. September 20: Laying of the foundation stone for the *Johannes Bau* (Goetheanum) in Dornach. Building begins immediately. The fourth Mystery Drama, *The Soul's Awakening* (CW 14), is completed. Also: *The Threshold of the Spiritual World* (CW 147). Lecture cycles include: *The Bhagavad Gita and the Epistles of Paul* and *The Esoteric Meaning of the Bhagavad Gita* (CW 146), which the Russian philosopher Nikolai Berdyaev attends; *The Mysteries of the East and of Christianity* (CW 144); *The Effects of Esoteric Development* (CW 145); and *The Fifth Gospel* (CW 148). In May, Rudolf Steiner is in London and Paris, where anthroposophical work continues.

1914: Building continues on the *Johannes Bau* (Goetheanum) in Dornach, with artists and co-workers from seventeen nations. The general assembly of the Anthroposophical Society takes place. In May, Rudolf Steiner visits Paris, as well as Chartres Cathedral. June 28: assassination in Sarajevo ('Now the catastrophe has happened!'). August 1: War is declared. Rudolf Steiner returns to Germany from Dornach—he will travel back and forth. He writes the last chapter of *The Riddles of Philosophy*. Lecture cycles include: *Human and Cosmic Thought* (CW 151); *Inner Being of Humanity between Death and a New Birth* (CW 153); *Occult Reading and Occult Hearing* (CW 156). December 24: marriage of Rudolf Steiner and Marie von Sivers.

1915: Building continues. Life after death becomes a major theme, also art. Writes: *Thoughts during a Time of War* (CW 24). Lectures include: *The Secret of Death* (CW 159); *The Uniting of Humanity through the Christ Impulse* (CW 165).

1916: Rudolf Steiner begins work with Edith Maryon (1872–1924) on the sculpture 'The Representative of Humanity' ('The Group'—Christ, Lucifer, and Ahriman). He also works with the alchemist Alexander von Bernus on the quarterly *Das Reich*. He writes *The Riddle of Humanity* (CW 20). Lectures include: *Necessity and Freedom in World History and Human Action* (CW 166); *Past and Present in the Human Spirit* (CW 167); *The Karma of Vocation* (CW 172); *The Karma of Untruthfulness* (CW 173).

1917: Russian Revolution. The U.S. enters the war. Building continues. Rudolf Steiner delineates the idea of the 'threefold nature of the human being' (in a public lecture March 15) and the 'threefold nature of the social organism' (hammered out in May–June with the help of Otto von Lerchenfeld and Ludwig Polzer-Hoditz in the form of two documents titled *Memoranda,* which were distributed in high places). August–September: Rudolf Steiner writes *The Riddles of the Soul* (CW 20). Also: commentary on 'The Chymical Wedding of Christian Rosenkreutz' for Alexander Bernus (Das *Reich*). Lectures include: *The Karma of Materialism* (CW 176); *The Spiritual Background of the Outer World: The Fall of the Spirits of Darkness* (CW 177).

1918: March 18: peace treaty of Brest-Litovsk—'Now everything will truly enter chaos! What is needed is cultural renewal.' June: Rudolf Steiner visits Karlstein (Grail) Castle outside Prague. Lecture cycle: *From Symptom to Reality in Modern History* (CW 185). In mid-November, Emil Molt, of the Waldorf-Astoria Cigarette Company, has the idea of founding a school for his workers' children.

1919: Focus on the threefold social organism: tireless travel, countless lectures, meetings, and publications. At the same time, a new public stage of Anthroposophy emerges as cultural renewal begins.

The coming years will see initiatives in pedagogy, medicine, pharmacology, and agriculture. January 27: threefold meeting: 'We must first of all, with the money we have, found free schools that can bring people what they need.' February: first public eurythmy performance in Zurich. Also: 'Appeal to the German People' (CW 24), circulated March 6 as a newspaper insert. In April, *Towards Social Renewal* (CW 23) appears—'perhaps the most widely read of all books on politics appearing since the war'. Rudolf Steiner is asked to undertake the 'direction and leadership' of the school founded by the Waldorf-Astoria Company. Rudolf Steiner begins to talk about the 'renewal' of education. May 30: a building is selected and purchased for the future Waldorf School. August–September, Rudolf Steiner gives a lecture course for Waldorf teachers, *The Foundations of Human Experience (Study of Man)* (CW 293). September 7: Opening of the first Waldorf School. December (into January): first science course, the *Light Course* (CW 320).

1920: The Waldorf School flourishes. New threefold initiatives. Founding of limited companies *Der Kommende Tag* and *Futurum A.G.* to infuse spiritual values into the economic realm. Rudolf Steiner also focuses on the sciences. Lectures: *Introducing Anthroposophical Medicine* (CW 312); *The Warmth Course* (CW 321); *The Boundaries of Natural Science* (CW 322); *The Redemption of Thinking* (CW 74). February: Johannes Werner Klein—later a co-founder of The Christian Community—asks Rudolf Steiner about the possibility of a 'religious renewal,' a 'Johannine church.' In March, Rudolf Steiner gives the first course for doctors and medical students. In April, a divinity student asks Rudolf Steiner a second time about the possibility of religious renewal. September 27–October 16: anthroposophical 'university course.' December: lectures titled *The Search for the New Isis* (CW 202).

1921: Rudolf Steiner continues his intensive work on cultural renewal, including the uphill battle for the threefold social order. 'University' arts, scientific, theological, and medical courses include: *The Astronomy Course* (CW 323); *Observation, Mathematics, and Scientific Experiment* (CW 324); the *Second Medical Course* (CW 313); *Colour*. In June and September–October, Rudolf Steiner also gives the first two 'priests' courses' (CW 342 and 343). The 'youth movement' gains momentum. Magazines are founded: *Die Drei* (January), and—under the editorship of Albert Steffen (1884–1963)—the weekly, *Das Goetheanum* (August). In February–March, Rudolf Steiner takes his first trip outside Germany since the war (Holland). On April 7, Steiner receives a letter regarding 'religious renewal,' and May 22–23, he agrees to address the question in a practical way. In June, the Klinical-Therapeutic Institute opens in Arlesheim under the direction of Dr Ita Wegman. In August, the

Chemical-Pharmaceutical Laboratory opens in Arlesheim (Oskar Schmiedel and Ita Wegman are directors). The Clinical Therapeutic Institute is inaugurated in Stuttgart (Dr Ludwig Noll is director); also the Research Laboratory in Dornach (Ehrenfried Pfeiffer and Gunther Wachsmuth are directors). In November–December, Rudolf Steiner visits Norway.

1922: The first half of the year involves very active public lecturing (thousands attend); in the second half, Rudolf Steiner begins to withdraw and turn toward the Society—'The Society is asleep.' It is 'too weak' to do what is asked of it. The businesses—*Der Kommende Tag* and *Futurum A.G.*—fail. In January, with the help of an agent, Steiner undertakes a twelve-city German lecture tour, accompanied by eurythmy performances. In two weeks he speaks to more than 2,000 people. In April, he gives a 'university course' in The Hague. He also visits England. In June, he is in Vienna for the East–West Congress. In August–September, he is back in England for the Oxford Conference on Education. Returning to Dornach, he gives the lectures *Philosophy, Cosmology, and Religion* (CW 215), and gives the third priests' course (CW 344). On September 16, The Christian Community is founded. In October–November, Steiner is in Holland and England. He also speaks to the youth: *The Youth Course* (CW 217). In December, Steiner gives lectures titled *The Origins of Natural Science* (CW 326), and *Humanity and the World of Stars: The Spiritual Communion of Humanity* (CW 219). December 31: Fire at the Goetheanum, which is destroyed.

1923: Despite the fire, Rudolf Steiner continues his work unabated. A very hard year. Internal dispersion, dissension, and apathy abound. There is conflict—between old and new visions—within the Society. A wake-up call is needed, and Rudolf Steiner responds with renewed lecturing vitality. His focus: the spiritual context of human life; initiation science; the course of the year; and community building. As a foundation for an artistic school, he creates a series of pastel sketches. Lecture cycles: *The Anthroposophical Movement; Initiation Science* (CW 227) (in Wales at the Penmaenmawr Summer School); *The Four Seasons and the Archangels* (CW 229); *Harmony of the Creative Word* (CW 230); *The Supersensible Human* (CW 231), given in Holland for the founding of the Dutch Society. On November 10, in response to the failed Hitler-Ludendorff putsch in Munich, Steiner closes his Berlin residence and moves the *Philosophisch-Anthroposophisch Verlag* (Press) to Dornach. On December 9, Steiner begins the serialization of his *Autobiography: The Course of My Life* (CW 28) in *Das Goetheanum*. It will continue to appear weekly, without a break, until his death. Late December–early January: Rudolf Steiner re-founds the Anthroposophical Society (about 12,000 members internationally) and takes over its leadership. The new board members are: Marie Steiner, Ita Wegman, Albert Steffen, Elisabeth Vreede, and Gunther Wachsmuth. (See *The Christmas Meeting for the Founding of the General Anthroposophical Society*, CW 260.) Accompanying lectures: *Mystery Knowledge and Mystery Centres* (CW 232); *World History in the Light of Anthroposophy* (CW 233). December 25: the Foundation Stone is laid (in the hearts of members) in the form of the 'Foundation Stone Meditation.'

1924: January 1: having founded the Anthroposophical Society and taken over its leadership, Rudolf Steiner has the task of 'reforming' it. The process begins with a weekly newssheet ('What's Happening in the Anthroposophical Society') in which Rudolf Steiner's 'Letters to Members' and 'Anthroposophical Leading Thoughts' appear (CW 26). The next step is the creation of a new esoteric class, the 'first class' of the 'University of Spiritual Science' (which was to have been followed, had Rudolf Steiner lived longer, by two more advanced classes). Then comes a new language for Anthroposophy—practical, phenomenological, and direct; and Rudolf Steiner creates the model for the second Goetheanum. He begins the series of extensive 'karma' lectures (CW 235–40); and finally, responding to needs, he creates two new initiatives: biodynamic agriculture and curative education. After the middle of the year, rumours begin to circulate regarding Steiner's health. Lectures: January–February, *Anthroposophy* (CW 234); February: *Tone Eurythmy* (CW 278); June: *The Agriculture Course* (CW 327); June–July: *Speech Eurythmy* (CW 279); *Curative Education* (CW 317); August: (England, 'Second International Summer School'), *Initiation Consciousness: True and False Paths in Spiritual Investigation* (CW 243); September: *Pastoral Medicine* (CW 318). On September 26, for the first time, Rudolf Steiner cancels a lecture. On September 28, he gives his last lecture. On September 29, he withdraws to his studio in the carpenter's shop; now he is definitively ill. Cared for by Ita Wegman, he continues working, however, and writing the weekly instalments of his *Autobiography* and *Letters to the Members/Leading Thoughts* (CW 26).

1925: Rudolf Steiner, while continuing to work, continues to weaken. He finishes *Extending Practical Medicine* (CW 27) with Ita Wegman. On March 30, around ten in the morning, Rudolf Steiner dies.

Index

Steiner

A NOTE FROM RUDOLF STEINER PRESS

We are an independent publisher and registered charity (non-profit organisation) dedicated to making available the work of Rudolf Steiner in English translation. We care a great deal about the content of our books and have hundreds of titles available – as printed books, ebooks and in audio formats.

As a publisher devoted to anthroposophy...

- We continually commission translations of previously unpublished works by Rudolf Steiner and invest in re-translating, editing and improving our editions.
- We are committed to making anthroposophy available to all by publishing introductory books as well as contemporary research.
- Our new print editions and ebooks are carefully checked and proofread for accuracy, and converted into all formats for all platforms.
- Our translations are officially authorised by Rudolf Steiner's estate in Dornach, Switzerland, to whom we pay royalties on sales, thus assisting their critical work.

So, look out for Rudolf Steiner Press as a mark of quality and support us today by buying our books, or contact us should you wish to sponsor specific titles or to support the charity with a gift or legacy.

office@rudolfsteinerpress.com
Join our e-mailing list at www.rudolfsteinerpress.com

RUDOLF STEINER PRESS